Coordinating English at Key Stage 1

Jenny Tyrrell and Narinderjit Gill

FALMER PRESS
· Taylor & Francis Group ·

First published 2000
by Falmer Press
11 New Fetter Lane, London EC4P 4EE

Simultaneously published in the USA and Canada
by Falmer Press
Garland Inc, 19 Union Square West, New York, NY 10003

Falmer Press is an imprint of the Taylor & Francis Group

© 2000 Jenny Tyrrell and Narinderjit Gill

The right of Jenny Tyrrell and Narinderjit Gill to be identified as the
Author of this Work has been asserted by them in accordance with
the Copyright, Designs and Patents Act 1988

Typeset in Melior by Graphicraft Limited, Hong Kong
Printed and bound in Great Britain by T.J. International,
Padstow, Cornwall

British Library Cataloguing in Publication Data
A catalogue record for this book is available from the British Library

Library of Congress Cataloging in Publication Data
A catalogue record for this book has been requested

ISBN 0-7507-0685-6

Contents

Acknowledgments   viii
Series editor's preface   ix
Introduction   I
English coordinator or literacy coordinator?   I

Part one
The role of the English coordinator at Key Stage I

Chapter I What is the role of the coordinator?   5

Chapter 2 Being a coordinator   8
Establishing your role   8
Getting started   10
Planning for success   16
Providing experiences of literacy   19
Modelling lessons — using Big Books   24
Using story (Yr 2)   47
Staffroom noticeboards   48
Sharing the curriculum initiative   50

Chapter 3 Strategies for staff development   57
Organising Inset   57
Learning to manage meetings   62

Part two
what you need to know about English and literacy at Key Stage I

Chapter 4 Establishing basic beliefs about literacy   69
Basic beliefs   69
Key Statement I: The foundations of literacy are laid at home
   in the early years   72

Key Statement 2: We can build on those early foundations   77
Key Statement 3: The children need a language rich
    environment   80
Key Statement 4: All reading and writing experiences should be
    child centred, purposeful and meaningful   83

Chapter 5 How does all this fit within the Literacy
    Framework?   94
Reinforcing practice   94
Links with other subjects   97
Children with English as an additional language   101
Children with special needs   103

Part three
Developing and maintaining a policy for English at Key Stage 1

Chapter 6 Producing a policy document   109
Why do we need a policy document for English?   109
Where to begin?   110
What to include?   111
Presenting the policy document   122
The policy as a vehicle for staff development   124
Relationship to the School Development Plan   125

Chapter 7 Planning   126
Where do we start?   128
Medium-term planning   128
And so to the short term   131
What about areas outside literacy?   134

Part four
Monitoring for quality

Chapter 8 Assessment   141
Why do we do it?   141
When to do assessment   143
Assessment opportunities   144
Assessment during the Literacy Hour   145

Chapter 9 Baseline assessment   151
Getting the Baseline and setting the target   151
Looking at Baselines . . . starting points   152
Target setting using SAT results   155

Chapter 10 Evidence of achievement at Key Stage 1   160
Children's achievements in reading   160
Children's achievements in writing   166
Children's achievements in speaking and listening   172
Evaluating the data   174
The use of portfolios   177
Storing the data   179
Reporting to parents   180
Reporting to the junior department   183
Successful schools   183

Part five
Resources for learning

Chapter 11 Managing resources and facilities   187
Resources for children   187
Funding   192
Resources for teachers   193
A final word, or two   193

References   195
Big Books   197
Index   198

Acknowledgments

Thanks are extended to:
Emma Stephenson
Janice Wrigley
Joy McCormick and
Kalwinder Randhawa.

Many of the examples of children's and teachers' work in this book come from their work as support teachers on the 'Quality Start' project in Sandwell LEA.

In particular, thanks to the contribution of work developed by Joy McCormick on assessment which we are sure teachers will find invaluable (pp. 142–5).

Quality Start is a partnership between Sandwell Primary schools, Sandwell LEA and the Education Development Unit at St Martins College, Ambleside. It is funded through the Single Regeneration Budget. The project has successfully supported the work of schools by helping teachers develop their expertise, skills and effectiveness in the classroom in order to raise standards of achievements. Therefore a special thanks to all the teachers and consultants that have been involved in making it a success in Sandwell.

Our thanks also to Mick Waters for bringing us together to write this book and for his help and advice.

Series editor's preface

This book has been prepared for primary teachers charged with the responsibility of acting as coordinators for English at Key Stage 1. It forms part of a series of new publications that set out to advise such teachers on the complex issues of improving teaching and learning through managing each element of the primary school curriculum.

Why is there a need for such a series? Most authorities recognise, after all, that the quality of primary children's work and learning depends upon the skills of their class teacher, not in the structure of management systems, sagacity of the policy documents or the titles and job descriptions of members of staff. Many today recognise that school improvement equates directly to the improvement of teaching, so surely all tasks, other than imparting subject knowledge, are merely a distraction for the committed primary teacher.

Nothing should take teachers away from their most important role, that is, serving the best interests of the class of children in their care and this book, and the others in the series, does not wish to diminish that mission. However, the increasing complexity of the primary curriculum and society's expanding expectations, make it very difficult for the class teacher to keep up to date with every development. Within traditional subject areas there has been an explosion of knowledge and new fields introduced such as science, technology, design, problem solving and health education, not to mention the uses of computers. These are now considered entitlements for primary children. Furthermore, we now expect all children to succeed at these studies, not just the fortunate few. All this has overwhelmed a class teacher system largely unchanged since the inception of primary schools.

Primary class teachers cannot possibly be expert in every aspect of the curriculum they are required to teach. To whom can they turn for help? It is unrealistic to assume that such support will be available from the headteacher whose responsibilities have grown ever wider since the 1988 Educational Reform Act. Constraints, including additional staff costs, and the loss of benefits from the strength and security of the class teacher system, militate against wholesale adoption of specialist or semi-specialist teaching. Help therefore has to come from exploiting the talents of teachers themselves, in a process of mutual support. Hence, primary schools have chosen many and varied systems of consultancy or subject coordination which best suit the needs of their children and the current expertise of the staff.

In fact, curriculum leadership functions in primary schools have increasingly been shared with class teachers through the policy of curriculum coordination for the past twenty years, especially to improve the consistency of work in language and mathematics. Since then each school has developed their own system and the series recognises that the system each reader is part of will be a compromise between the ideal and the possible. Campbell and Neill (1994) show that by 1991 nearly nine out of every ten primary class teachers had such responsibility and the average number of subjects each was between 1.5 and 2.2 (depending on the size of school).

These are the people for whom this series sets out to help to do this part of their work. The books each deal with specific issues whilst at the same time providing an overview of general themes in the management of the subject curriculum. The term *subject leader* is used in an inclusive sense and combines the two major roles that such teachers play when they have responsibility for subjects and aspects of the primary curriculum.

The books each deal with:

- **coordination**: a role which emphasises harmonising, bringing together, making links, establishing routines and common practice; and,
- **subject leadership**: a role which emphasises: providing information, offering expertise and direction, guiding the development of the subject, and raising standards.

The purpose of the series is to give practical guidance and support to teachers — in particular what to do and how to do it. They each offer help on the production, development and review of policies and schemes of work; the organisation of resources, and developing strategies for improving the management of the subject curriculum.

Each book in the series contains material that subject managers will welcome and find useful in developing their subject expertise and in tackling problems of enthusing and motivating staff.

Each book has five parts:

1 The review and development of the different roles coordinators are asked to play.
2 Updating subject knowledge and subject pedagogical knowledge.
3 Developing and maintaining policies and schemes of work.
4 Monitoring work within the school to enhance the continuity of teaching and progression in pupil's learning.
5 Resources and contacts.

The advice is practical; the aim is high. This book will help readers to develop both the subject expertise they will need and the managerial perspective necessary to enthuse and inform others.

Mike Harrison, Series Editor
May 1999

Introduction

English coordinator or literacy coordinator?

With the government's interest in literacy standards so prominent in our thinking, this book focuses upon the issues directly related to the acquisition of literacy skills. Most teachers agree that this should be the main focus of our teaching in the classroom for young children. The importance of developing the ability to read and write has always been the priority for infant teachers. With the introduction of a fuller, statutory curriculum at Key Stage 1, some teachers conscientiously introduced the wider and more complete programmes of study into their classrooms without having the confidence to use the potential for each subject area as a vehicle for the teaching of literacy skills. The content of the subjects became the driving force and teachers clung on to the complexity of completing the curriculum required rather than using it to support their work.

It has become obvious that many schools were so concerned with making sense of the requirements and implementing the National Curriculum, that the real focus of our work was diluted as teachers came to terms with attainment targets and level descriptors that were revised and slimmed down to help us, just as they were being understood. There was so much to absorb and learn and very many experienced, thorough, competent teachers felt their confidence shaken. They concentrated upon the new things that they had to learn in order to survive.

Knowledge and development about reading was almost put on hold with an outlook that said, 'We're doing that anyway, so let's concentrate on what we don't understand'.

Other subjects were to eat into the time available and the threat of inspection meant that many schools were constructing curriculum plans to ensure coverage rather than depth and coherence, with a resulting lack of progression for many children. This lack of progression made its most significant mark in some schools in the area of English.

Some schools managed to keep the emphasis upon literacy and developed strategies for coping with demands. They were the schools with the shared vision, consistent approaches, good planning, knowledgeable subject leaders and effective headteachers. In this book the emphasis is upon these aspects of teaching and school management within the context of English.

The Literacy Framework puts the focus firmly back upon English. The notion of the Literacy Hour sets the expectation that the subject cannot be 'on the list' and done when possible or if we think it is worth it. It has to happen; we have to learn how to teach literacy as opposed to simply organise for reading and writing to happen. But the Literacy Strategy goes further than this by expecting that children will experience literacy in many guises, including a national year of reading. So the hour of literacy is only part of the picture; the concentrated, direct teaching. Beyond this the school has to use other subject areas and activities, throughout the rest of the day as a springboard for extending and developing literacy experiences in context.

This book explores the way that the curriculum coordinator for English can have maximum influence upon children's learning. Some schools have appointed a literacy coordinator, sometimes in addition to the one for English, and this emphasises the school's commitment by concentrating upon the thrust of the new short-term strategy without losing the overall long-term view of English. Either way the book will offer guidance, suggestions and examples to coordinators at different career stages as they try to move the work of the schools forward.

Part one

The role of the English coordinator at KS 1

Chapter 1
What is the role of the coordinator?

Chapter 2
Being a coordinator

Chapter 3
Strategies for staff development

Chapter 1   What is the role of the coordinator?

Of all the jobs in the primary school, the role of coordinator for English at Key Stage 1 has the potential for enormous satisfaction and fulfilment. There are so many exciting stages in the early development of the child; the first cry, smile and step are memorable, but the child's ability to understand and use language is probably the greatest achievement. It is the one that gives us a real insight into the way a child is thinking.

In school young children's early attempts to express themselves in, and understand, the written form can give the same sense of excited pleasure to those involved. The squiggles on the page with left to right orientation. The indecipherable, yet recognisable shopping list or telephone message. The first attempts at independent reading when the child displays an understanding that reading a text gives meaning, even though the spoken and written words contain the gist but no print/word accuracy.

To be involved at this early stage as a class teacher is exciting, to be English coordinator for Key Stage 1 and to have responsibility for the structuring of language development in young children is indeed a role to treasure. An intrinsic motivation, a sense of wonder at the enormity of what the majority of children achieve after the first two years of formal schooling has to be at the heart of the good early years English coordinator. They should possess the awareness to observe constantly and learn from the many different ways that children

- extend their vocabulary;
- develop an ability to express themselves orally;
- become readers and transfer their thoughts into the written form.

It should be a person who refers to published research in an attempt to find answers, thus further enlightening and informing knowledge of the learning processes involved; someone who is likely to be a person who will influence the thinking of others. These are the strengths needed to motivate and lead staff in order to improve the quality of the education our children receive. It is these qualities of observation and inquiry, of interest and enthusiasm that will give you, the English coordinator, the strength to inspire, encourage, support and guide those around them.

However, it should be emphasised that this is a role with heavy responsibility, for the acquisition of literacy in particular is an area of priority for parents and society. Their concerns and worries can have a direct effect on the way teachers perform and on the progress of the children.

The role of coordination in the primary school has changed dramatically over the years from the position where three or four people had responsibility posts for key areas of the curriculum, to the situation today where every member of staff is expected to take such responsibility, however inexperienced they might be, in addition to their responsibility to the children in their class.

The Teacher Training Agency has set standards of responsibility for different levels within the profession and included are the expectations for 'subject leaders'. In an ideal world we would have primary schools with a suitably informed and experienced teacher capable of taking on such leadership in each subject area. As time goes on this will probably happen, but the reality of most schools is that there are often not enough teachers to cover the subjects and many people end up taking on two or more areas where they have no particular expertise. In the past the English coordination role was seen as one that anyone could do for there was an assumption that we had all received basic training. This was far from the truth, for quality time during teacher training, devoted solely to the acquisition of literacy, seems to have been missing. One still meets recently trained teachers who lack the knowledge and skills to lead children successfully into literacy, especially the 8- or 9-year-old struggler.

National standards of subject leadership have now been set and we must look positively to the future and find ways to attain these standards. The Teacher Training Agency identifies the *core purpose* of subject leadership, which is:

> *to provide professional leadership for a subject to secure high quality teaching and effective use of resources, and ensure improved standards of achievement for all pupils.*

What follows from this are some *key outcomes*:
- *for pupils*
- *for teachers*
- *for parents*
- *for senior management*
- *and for other adults*

The TTA then outlines four key *areas for development*:
1 *Strategic development of the subject*
2 *Teaching and learning*
3 *Leading and managing staff*
4 *Efficient and effective deployment of staff and resources*

The TTA then draws out the *skills and attributes* necessary to do the job. When you read the official document and tease out what it means you will find a distinct similarity with the issues addressed in this section. The job is complex and significant, especially when it is recognised that it needs to be done alongside the class teaching responsibility. This can, however, be used to advantage, for as English coordinator you have the opportunity to develop first class practice within your own classroom, where theory becomes practice and theory is developed from practice. This will give you credibility with colleagues. You, the English coordinator, are *doing it* and being seen to do it, not just telling others what to do.

Chapter 2   Being a coordinator

Establishing your role

How you establish your role will depend upon whether the appointment is in-house or you have come from another school. There are pros and cons for both situations and as English coordinator you need to exploit whichever situation you find yourself in.

Coming from outside

It is often easier to be a newcomer making a fresh start, establishing new relationships and bringing lots of knowledge and experience gained from your previous school. However, it will take longer for you to establish your role as you have to settle into a new environment.

Put down roots You will need at least a term to put down roots and settle into your classroom teaching, for whilst you are a teaching coordinator the children in your own class are your number one priority. Make your feelings on this matter known to the headteacher and at the very first staff meeting explain your viewpoint to the staff. Tell them that you need time to settle in and absorb the workings of the school and get the feel of the way things are done.

Socialise with colleagues You will need to get to know personalities, spot possible allies, note potentially troublesome

Suggestion

Establishing positive relationships

Pop into classrooms and comment on praiseworthy work that is displayed. Talk to teachers about their successes. Be as positive as you can whilst lending a sympathetic ear to genuine concerns. Build up relationships of trust and respect. It may be that a member of the present staff also applied for the post, there might be hard feelings and pockets of allegiance. You need a thick skin and a confidence in your own worth to weather possible cold fronts.

elements, and the way to do that is to talk to different groups regularly. Genuinely get to know people.

Find out as much as you can about their lives without being intrusive. If someone is experiencing severe personal problems it is as well to know because their reactions to new initiatives may well be influenced by these factors. Be prepared to share something of yourself too: let people get to know you, discuss your particular interests.

Other coordinators You need to develop a good working relationship with other members of the management team. This is all to do with establishing allies for the future as you will undoubtedly need the backing and support of like-minded people in the future. This is a reciprocal arrangement because they will undoubtedly need your support too. It is also good to have a united, committed, team approach to issues within the school.

The headteacher It goes without saying that you need to develop a harmonious working relationship with the headteacher. This is someone who has put a lot of trust in you, it is up to you to prove that the right choice was made.

The children You need to get to know the children in the school. Talk to them about things to do with English when you are on playground duty. Ask them what they are reading, talk about books, ask if they have done any really good pieces of writing lately, encourage them to bring good work to show you. Establish yourself in the eyes of the children as a person who cares deeply about the subject. Become the 'English' person about the school but try not to be the only one who can sort out the issues; you want a whole school commitment.

The secretary There will be occasions when you need a letter sent out in a hurry, extra photocopying done, etc. Time spent developing a friendly relationship with office staff is a must.

The caretaker/cleaning staff These are very important people to have a good relationship with in the school. There will be times when you will need help getting ready for a display, a curriculum evening for parents etc. You don't want to upset fixed routines but will have to find ways to gain their willing compliance if your actions affect their jobs.

Being appointed from within the school

An in-house appointment means that you have already proved your worth in the eyes of the headteacher and senior management team and are seen to be the right person for the job. It can however bring hidden problems in as much as everyone knows you, warts and all. A few warts are not necessarily a bad thing. A superstar is not always the best person to lead others who are less sure of their abilities. They can make the weak feel even more inadequate.

Presumably you will already have allies, like-minded people who will lend support when new initiatives are being put into place. . . . but beware, you never know when a personal friend with a different point of view will become a problem. Again, a thick skin and a lot of tact are needed – qualities that aren't always easy to muster in a meeting at the end of a long and possibly stress-filled day dealing with young children.

Take stock Whatever the situation of the appointment you need to settle down and take stock. Don't rush into things too quickly. What you have to do is select an area of improvement for your first initiative that is not too ambitious, is relevant and that is assured of success.

Getting started

Job description

This might seem a bit simplistic, but you really do need to know exactly what is expected of you. Inheriting a job description written years before might not suit your particular strengths. It is a good idea to negotiate your role once you have settled into the school.

You know you have responsibility for English, but the level of overall responsibility needs discussion. As Key Stage 1 coordinator you may be in a separate infant/Key Stage 1/lower school unit with total control of the department. You might be one of a team of English coordinators in a big school and have to liaise with the Key Stage 2 coordinator. Do you have equal status? Is one role more senior than the other? There are so many overlapping roles within a school with the potential for misunderstanding and conflict to develop that these issues need to be addressed.

It could be that your level of responsibility will change as you grow into the role, which seems a sensible approach. Perhaps at first you will be answerable to the lower school coordinator/head of infants. As you mature in the job or staffing changes occur so will the dynamics of the management team. The needs of the school and your position within it will vary.

It is interesting to read the wider literature on management issues, not just educational management. Torrington and Hall (1987) in their book entitled *Personnel Management: A New Approach*, emphasise this need for goal clarity. 'Is the person fully aware of the job requirements?' It's no good reaching a crisis point and having someone tell you that you were supposed to organise a seemingly unrelated item because of some obscure historical precedent.

They also emphasise the question, 'does the person have the capacity to do the job well?' The job description for many English coordinators is way beyond their current capabilities and they waste many hours struggling with feelings of inadequacy before good sense returns and they realise that there is no way that they could instantly do all that is required. Often job descriptions are written in a rush by the previous postholder who describes the job *as they left it* not from where they began 'x' number of years ago. As we all get more experienced it is all too easy to forget what it was like at the beginning.

Once you have settled in, talk with your headteacher and negotiate a role description that you are both happy with. Agree to review and extend it after a period of time.

Suggestion

More insights into the management role can be found in Wilson (1992) entitled *A Strategy of Change*, a book relating to corporate management but with relevance for all organisations, including schools. He discusses the insight that people tend to stick to what they know and use it as a template for future decisions. He refers to the work of Lindblom who back in 1959 wrote a paper entitled 'The science of muddling through' ... that sounds like a very familiar concept! Lindblom suggested that there is a process of 'incrementalism' whereby we build out from the current situation in small steps and by small degrees.

The next step is to be sure that colleagues know the nature of your role so that they have a realistic understanding of your input into school life.

It all seems so very obvious and yet as Michael Fullan (1991) cites, the history of educational change is everywhere littered with big, top-down, politically motivated changes that swamp teachers and produce the inevitable pattern of hysterical response.

This is one reason why the Literacy Strategy creates its own problems. It is a fine idea for teachers throughout the country to focus on one really important issue. The thinking behind the Literacy Strategy shows a genuine concern for improving the standards achieved by children by improving the quality of teaching. The challenge lies in the implementation. Teachers need to be convinced that the initiative is not simply a criticism of their previous efforts to help children acquire literacy skills. An initiative of this type should be greeted with enthusiasm as it provides everyone with the opportunity to work together for the good of future children. We as teachers should have imprinted on our brains 'start from where the learner is'. We need to keep that to the fore when planning changes with colleagues. What happens so often is that teachers are all fired up to do new things with children who are not necessarily ready for such drastic changes. Prepare the children as well as the teachers.

Conducting an audit

During that first settling-in term, start with an audit. Take a copy of the school policy for English, if there is one, and by walking about the school and talking to people, discover how well the written word matches with the reality of what is going on.

Look at the key areas of the English curriculum. The following are some simple starting points.

Is there evidence that children are actively engaged in situations to extend their listening and speaking, reading and writing skills?

- Who does the most talking, teacher or children?
- Are the children working individually or are they working as a group to solve problems?
- Are the classrooms a print-rich environment in which the children will develop literacy skills?
- Do teachers display a wide variety of texts including fiction, stories and poems, and non-fiction at a suitable level for the children to browse through?
- Are books a focal, eye catching part of the classroom?
- If there is a book corner does it invite children to curl up with a book?
- How often does the teacher spend time with the individual reader?
- Are the children given specific, concentrated skills demonstrations with the teacher modelling reading and writing?
- Is there evidence of the use of poetry and rhyme to develop phonemic awareness?
- How often do books go home with the children?
- Is there some kind of dialogue card or book for the parents to comment on the books that go home?
- Is there a consistent approach to the emergence of early writing?
- Are children encouraged to write with a variety of pencils, pens, paper types, colours and sizes?
- Is handwriting and correct letter formation taught in a systematic and consistent way in all classrooms?
- Do the teachers follow the agreed policy for the teaching of spelling or is it assumed it will be 'caught'?
- Are the children encouraged to use computers for writing, individually and as pairs, sharing ideas and knowledge?
- Is there evidence that the children are involved in role play and drama activities?
- Is there evidence of connections and links between the language strands to enable the young child to see the whole literacy picture?
- Do the teachers exploit the whole curriculum as a vehicle for literacy acquisition?

Talk to the children, they'll tell you what you need to know. Look at the work they are doing:

- is it motivating?
- is it stretching them?
- do they have pride in what they are doing?
- do they know why they are doing it?
- are there high expectations of what they can achieve?

Analyse the pupil records:
- is it an efficient system?
- do they really tell you about the child as a developing learner?
- do teachers consult them or just fill them in a day or two before they have to be given in?

Have a look at the resources:
- are resources regarded as the property of the school or the individual who ordered them?
- do staff who have been there a long time have well-equipped rooms and newer staff sparse resources?
- is a clear out needed?
- what do you need to buy?

Then talk with the headteacher again and plan a strategy highlighting priority areas. Start small and start from where the school is.

Small steps and small degrees

Perhaps you have a worry that the staff do not have a wide knowledge of the variety of books that are available for the young reader nowadays. They might know about story books but what about poetry and non-fiction? Take as your starting point something that is completely unthreatening to anyone. Easier said than done you might say, but this is where English is such a good responsibility area for there are so many ways to promote good practice.

Activity 1

Why not start with a really eye-catching book display? Put it in a prominent position in the school to show the importance of the event, not in the cloakroom behind the coats. The entrance lobby is a good place. Start by involving the children, who will then involve their teachers. Put on a display of 'A Really Good Book'. Ask the children to decide on perhaps ten books per class, they can be books found in school or books children enjoy at home, and get some written comments to accompany the texts. They don't have to be physically written by the very small children, but typed in big letters. Try to find time to take some photographs of children engrossed in books and get them blown up. Encourage the teachers to take their classes to visit the display. Leave it there for a week or so and then take it down. There's nothing worse than a display that once was good but is now covered in dust, so be aware of the life expectancy of such a venture.

Then follow up with a display by teachers and parents of 'The Books We Enjoyed When We Were Small'. This sort of activity involves children and parents and teachers in a celebration of reading. Start on a positive vein, get good things established before you start influencing your colleagues' awareness of new texts suitable for emerging readers and perhaps more importantly how they use them in the classroom. This sort of thing is a safe way into issues connected with reading.

Another idea is to focus on correct letter formation and print awareness. A young child's name is one of the most important things he or she owns. It is also one of our most valuable teaching tools. Their name is often the first word they learn to read and to write, so let's get rid of bats and balls, teddies and trains next to coat pegs and write the child's name clearly for them to recognise.

Then, include all the children, all the teachers and all the parents in a blitz on correct letter formation of the letters in the child's own name. In years to come unless Clare, aged 5 or 6, breaks the practice of beginning all the letters in her name at the bottom, she will have immense problems correcting this habit and c's and l's and a's and r's and e's will be a continual battle for her and her teachers.

Activity 2

Class by class arrange a display about 'Our Names', plus drawings of themselves. Encourage children to look for patterns in their name. I once knew a little boy who used to introduce himself as 'a strawberry jam sandwich' because he was BEN with JAM IN. Children love to look for patterns in their names. The children could be encouraged to think of other things they like that begin with the letters in their names. All good stuff for encouraging correct letter formation, print awareness, phonic knowledge and an awareness of letter strings and patterns. It is an excellent forerunner for a concerted effort on print awareness with young learners and a consistent approach to the importance of correct letter formation.

■ Starting with the children is a very good way to begin a working relationship with their teachers.
■ Involving the parents in early promotional projects will establish your commitment and reputation before you

embark on curriculum evenings about possibly controversial and difficult issues.
■ Starting with small projects that promote English will strengthen your position with colleagues and shouldn't upset anyone.

Planning for success

When planning your first major initiative, involve the staff. Send round a short questionnaire asking them to prioritise areas that they would like to focus on. The chances are they will be only too aware of the key issues.

When you have decided on your priority, talk with the headteacher or Key Stage 1 coordinator and negotiate an agreed starting point. Then, spend some time working on that area with your own class. Display the results and see if there are any favourable comments. If someone picks up on what you are doing then involve them. Suggest that they should try the approach and give you feedback. In this way you have a developing pilot test of the new initiative in place before it is introduced to staff.

The following case study is useful as a way of illustrating the issues. This English coordinator, in her initial audit, was aware that there did not seem to be enough emphasis placed on skills training in early reading and writing activities. She could not see any use of 'modelling' going on in the classrooms visited. Big Books were in evidence but the full 'teaching potential' of these enlarged texts did not appear to be exploited. Children could be seen sitting in a group, sharing experiences orally, but teachers modelling the writing of those events did not appear to take place. The coordinator therefore introduced a small wooden easel into her classroom. An invaluable piece of teaching equipment that in Australia and New Zealand has been in evidence for years.

Its advantages are many:
■ In a crowded infant classroom it can be stored behind the teacher's chair and brought out when needed.
■ It is light and safe to use with young children.

- All, or groups of children, can sit around the easel and clearly see both the text and the pictures.
- The teacher has two hands free to point to the words and invite response from the children through gesture.
- It is also wonderful for modelling writing. Sheets of paper can be pegged to the top and the whole group can be involved in composing sentences.
- To accompany the easel, teachers can have a selection of coloured pens of different thickness and intensity of colour. For example a fluorescent pen can be used to highlight key areas of grammar, or spelling patterns, after the writing is completed.
- The book or the piece of writing can be left on the easel for children to study individually. What often happens in infant classrooms is that one child will role play being the teacher thus reinforcing the learning for everyone involved.

When a Big Book was used, the children not only sat down to enjoy a good story, but they also sat down to learn about the business of reading.

Case study

The English coordinator used Joy Cowley's amusing story about *Mrs Wishy Washy*. The book was visited a number of times.
- The first reading allowed the children to relax and enjoy the story and the illustrations. (Children loved it and enjoyed experiencing the story over and over again, especially the page where the pig goes in the tub with his very bare, human-like bottom hanging over the edge.)

- On the second reading the teacher takes the story more slowly, page by page, focusing the children's attention specifically on the print.

'Oh, lovely mud,'
said the cow,
and she jumped in it.

- The children's attention is drawn to the squiggles that are speech marks. The way 'oh' is spelt with an 'h' on the end, that 'lovely' is love with 'ly' on the end, the 'y' making an 'ee' sound. That 'she' has two letters together that make a new sound 'sh' as in shoe, shop, shake etc.

- On turning over: 'Who can read the first line?' 'It's the same as on the previous page' 'Let's look for other patterns in the story'. Challenging the children to be observant. Focusing their eyes on the letters and words.

- On the third reading the children do it all by themselves.

- Then the book is left on the easel for groups of children to return and read it together, hunting for patterns, counting repeated words, helping each other and reinforcing their learning.

This small easel is also used for children to sit around whilst the teacher models writing. Teachers need to be active writers in the classroom in order to teach the children the skills at first hand. They need to take a shared experience and transfer it into text, showing the children how it is done in very concentrated teaching, including:
- Searching for a good opening sentence together.
- Puzzling over spelling and punctuation.
- Making mistakes and crossing them out.
- Altering and changing until a satisfactory piece of writing is completed.
- Showing the children how writers write.

This writing is done on large sheets and clipped together to make a class Big Book about events of the week. In this way the children return to their own, familiar writing to extend their reading skills.

Shared stories can be written in this way, also factual texts, letters, lists, notices — the list is endless. By 'engaging' the children in the modelling process we help them to become writers. Children have to make some sense of the whole experience themselves. Look at the work of Brian Cambourne for further reading about the importance of 'engagement'.

The coordinator got this going in her own classroom and then encouraged a colleague who had expressed interest to try it. By the time the issue came up at a curriculum meeting, a successful pilot had been running in two classrooms.

She *could* have ordered enough easels for every classroom, explained the process and then said that she would like everyone to try it. This would have been a recipe for disaster, but one that our own personal enthusiasm often leads us into. We are so convinced of the merits of the initiative that we are in a way blinkered to the concerns of others. We must try very hard not to impose, but rather to look for volunteers.

What she did was to explain the process, backed up with references from recent texts, and then introduced colleague 'A' who had been trying it out in her room. A peer explaining how she organised the approach and commenting on the successes and mistakes in the learning experience is a far better way to influence colleagues than describing how it worked in your own classroom. The fact that you can do it is not much help to the less confident and more 'set in their ways' members of staff.

The coordinator then explained that there was money available if anyone else wished to have an easel. A gamble, but one that paid off because many hands went up.

Once the majority of staff members were regularly engaged in modelling then the time for consistency of approach within the school came. The remaining few teachers were invited to watch easel work in action before they were asked to include this activity in their daily teaching. This was a good forerunner to more extensive work on the way reading and writing were taught in the school.

Providing experiences of literacy

In this society children live in a print-rich world full of writing and writers; they are surrounded by print before they even begin to learn about writing in the more structured environment of school. We need to build on the early experiences children show in their play as they develop writing behaviour. One way is to look at the classroom and analyse the ways in which literacy is displayed.

Questions to ask in the classroom:
■ are there timetables/announcements/notices/labels/charts;
■ are they written by child or adult;
■ how much child-written or child-dictated work is there;
■ how old is it and who displayed it;
■ role play area — are there relevant and accessible literacy materials (notebook, order forms, cheque books etc.);

- do children initiate activities involving magazines, cookery books, lists, food labels, posters, who brings these in;
- are there spaces for reading and writing, and when are they used;
- how many non-reading scheme books and comics and newspapers are there;
- accessibility of pens, paper, pencils, envelopes, typewriter, computer?

The classteacher should be able to draw a ground plan of the classroom and explain to parents when and where their children would have the opportunity of observing and experiencing literacy.

Writers need experience of writing in different ways for different people. The more they write for others in a variety of contexts, the more proficient they will become at meeting the needs of their readers and if writing is accepted, acknowledged and responded to, children continue to write not just to communicate, but to give pleasure.

Activity 3: Emergent writing activities

Signing in at activities — clip boards and paper were placed at activities and the children signed in when they visited the activity.

Milk Time — the children signed to say whether they wanted milk or squash at break time.

Covering tables with paper and providing a variety of writing materials for group pictures and writing.

Writing area — Cover table with letter shapes so the children have them on view at all times.

Writing own labels for coat pegs, drawers, equipment.

Collect forms and booklets and put them in the writing area.

When writing the children write first and the adults scribe later.

Make books for the children to write in.

Writing outside — water writing on walls and pathways.

Introduce to as many play areas as possible.

Take home packs encouraging emergent writing.

Provide a display area for the children to display work themselves.

Activity 4: Environmental print — writing for a purpose

Children taken on print walk around the school, looking for examples of print.

Task
- children have to decide how they will label classroom — in pairs;
- children can first see what is labelled, and what isn't, e.g. window;
- children choose appropriate card and writing implement;
- child sounds it out and writes, teacher scribes, child copies;
- finished work is mounted and child blu-tacks on correct part of classroom.

Extension
Children bring something from home with print on it. This is then mounted onto a wall — our word wall — and used as a stimulus for learning. For example, where does it say cornflakes, can we find another word beginning with the same letter?

Modelling writing

You can show teachers how to model writing by doing it well in your own classroom. Model writing to children by thinking aloud. The main advantages about this are that it helps children in making decisions about:

- what to write;
- how to start;
- how to revise/edit their own/others' work;
- how to present their ideas or information;
- how to use the print environment in the classroom (word banks);
- how to write a new form of text.

Overall it is a useful way to teach children the processes through which writers work. When scribing for children you are in effect:

- gathering children's ideas;
- demonstrating to them how to record their ideas/ information/thoughts;
- modelling process of structuring and organising notes;
- writing from notes, transforming notes into sentences;
- encouraging children to contribute their ideas as the teacher scribes.

After modelling and writing with children it is important to reiterate the main teaching points: 'I feel really happy with this description'; 'Now list the main things I've included: a range of vocabulary, used adjectives correctly and written in sentences.'

This gives children a clear reference point for their own writing. If children are then reviewing their own or each other's writing it also provides them with a focus.

As an example of this sort of work, you could consider models used in the 'Teddy Bears' Picnic' activity that follows. The children experience different types of writing for different purposes and the context that they can relate to brings it alive.

Activity 5: Models of writing for 'Teddy Bears' Picnic'

1 All children received invitation. (A)

<u>Invitation</u>

<u>Ravinda</u> is invited to the OHW Teddy Bears' Picnic on Friday 27th June at 1.15pm on the school field.

R.S.V.P.

to Mrs Hickman or Mrs Wrigley (A)

2 The children wrote their reply on proforma. (B)

wednesday

Mrs Hickman

I am coming to the picnic on Friday 27th June at 1.15pm on the school field.

from Ravinda (B)

---

3   Then the children wrote own invitation to their teddy using (A) as a model.

4   The following letter (C) was displayed on class noticeboard to stimulate response.

Mrs Wrigley,

The other teddies told me last night about the picnic on 27th June.

They told me the picnic will be on the school field. I am worried about the weather because it rains quite often in Tividale.

Have you thought what you will do if it rains ? Will we all get wet ?

Perhaps the clever children in OHW will have some ideas. Let me know as soon as possible.

Love from,

Tyree's Teddy

 (C)

5   Children replied in this simple letter format.
6   Letter (D) was stimulus for children to write list of, and draw, suitable clothes for teddies.

Kipper and Floppy's group,

All the teddies are much happier now that we know what the plan will be if it rains on the day of the picnic. We did wonder if you could all help us with one last thing and that is what to wear for the picnic.

Perhaps you could make a list of clothes for us to choose from, and perhaps even decide on some colours too. If you leave the ideas by the blackboard we could look at them tonight.

Love from,

All the Teddies

 (D)

Modelling lessons — using Big Books

You can also model lessons to show teachers how to use Big Books effectively. The following case studies illustrate the potential for using Big Books within the classroom. Big Books are now being recognised by teachers as an effective resource for the Literacy Hour during the whole class shared reading and word level work. The case studies are taken from work carried out by advisory teachers in Sandwell on a raising standards project. Their lesson plans effectively illustrate the key teaching strategies and learning that takes place. They also highlight the importance of effective teacher questioning to not only probe children's knowledge and understanding but also challenge their thinking.

As a coordinator you will need to think carefully about the components of the Literacy Hour and in particular the first 30 minutes. The messages you give through the practice within your classroom will make a huge difference to the quality of tasks children are given. Teachers need to question the most appropriate place for the whole class work — whether the carpet is always the most effective place or whether using the desks and giving children a text highlighting task would fit better. It allows us to question the environment we want to create for learning that allows children to work better and develop a certain set of qualities. Finally, perhaps we should consider what resources children can be using during the whole class work — could they be jotting notes or text highlighting rather than sitting with nothing to do.

Case study I

Big Book — *Oscar Got the Blame* by Tony Ross

Learning outcomes
    Pupils will respond to the text in a variety of ways.
    Pupils will engage in a writing task.
    Pupils will share their responses with at least one other person.

Effective teaching
    Teacher questioning to encourage pupils to think about the book in detail.

Pupils will work in a variety of ways.
Use of paired discussion to encourage pupils to verbalise thoughts and feelings.
Use of time targets to structure pace of lesson.
Use of clear and explicit instructions to the pupils about what they are expected to do.

Resources:
Flip-chart paper; Cloze activities; 'Oscar' phonics book; A3 Oscars to use for descriptive words; Sheets to draw Billy; Big Book: *Oscar Got the Blame*.

Introduction ST
Show pupils the book which we are going to read today. Tell them that the title is covered because we are going to use the illustration on the front cover to try to predict what the book is going to be about.

Give them 30 seconds to talk to their friend about it. Feedback some ideas.

Now uncover the title. What does it say? Now what do we think the book is going to be about? The same as before or different? Give them 30 seconds more to talk to their friend.

Before reading the book ask:
    what is this called? (point to front cover)
    what are the pictures called?
    what is the name for the name of the book?

What do all these things give us clues about?

Support Teacher (ST) to read the book. Ensure the picture of Billy is covered up at the end. Re-read the book, this time the pupils can join in the sentence, 'Oscar got the blame'.

Now turn the pages of the book for a third time, not reading the words but asking the pupils to silently look at the illustrations, and try to imagine what Oscar is feeling, and what the other characters in the book, including Billy, look like.

Ask the children now to discuss with their partner all the characters in the book, who are they? Pupils may need to be told the meaning of 'characters'. Give them 1 minute then list them on the flip-chart.

Lesson development

Explain to the pupils that they are all going to be working on different tasks about the book we have just read. Tell them the amount of time they will have to complete their tasks and that just before we all come back together at the end of the lesson, there will be 5 minutes to talk to another person in the class, and share the work they have been doing.

Class Teacher (CT) to introduce and run through tasks

Task 1: Paired work

Cloze activities in two levels of difficulty. Pupils should work together to stick in the missing words. Explain to the children that they should be careful not to lose any of the words as there are no extra ones. Also that they should not stick any words down until they have all been placed on the sheet and checked either by a teacher or someone else on their table. When they have completed the sheet, they should read together. The less able may use a photocopy of the completed story to help them.

Task 2: Paired/individual work
What does Billy look like?
Pupils to discuss with a friend what they think Billy looks like, concentrating on the expression on his face. Draw what they think he looks like individually, and write some sentences about him.

Task 3: Flip-chart story, small group (6) ST to support
Pin the two sheets up about Oscar on the flip-chart. Read and think about the questions together. Teacher and pupils to brainstorm words around the pictures of Oscar. After this, the group should try to incorporate these words into a story about what Oscar is going to do now. What will he say/do to Billy? What will he say/do to his parents to convince them that Billy is real? Will he do anything good/naughty?

Task 4: Paired writing, CT to support
Pupils to discuss in pairs the story and then complete the writing frame about which bits they liked, which bits they disliked and what they think will happen next. Talk and agree with a partner why they think it will happen next.

Task 5: Individual extension task (p. 30)
Pupils to think of objects which begin with the letters which make up Oscar and draw and write them on the concertinaed book.

Just before the plenary session, stop the pupils at whatever point they are at, partner them up and give them 5 minutes to share what they have been doing.

Plenary: CT to lead
Bring children together.
The group doing the story task to read their story.
What have you learnt?
How did you do it?
How have we worked?
Did you enjoy the activities?

Easy

Billy	Billy	Billy	Billy	Billy
Oscar	Oscar	Oscar	Oscar	

Oscar got the blame...
got
the

'THEY NEVER DO!'

Hard

Billy	Billy	Billy	Billy	Billy	Billy
Oscar	Oscar	Oscar	Oscar		

Dad's
Granny's
got   got
blame   blame   blame
cat
the   the
said   said

'THEY NEVER DO!'

Task 2: Paired/individual work

This is Billy.....

Task 3: Oscar Got the Blame

What we like about the story.....

because...

What we like about the story....

because...

Oscar

What we think will happen next is.....

Task 5: Individual extension task

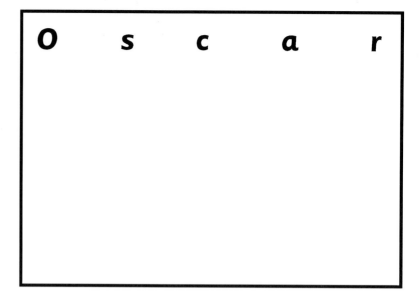

O s c a r

Case study 2

Big Book *Nursery Rhymes*

Learning outcomes
Learn, re-read and recite favourite poems, taking account of punctuation; to comment on aspects such as word combinations, sound patterns (such as rhymes, rhythms . . .) . . . Yr 2: T. 1 Investigate and classify words with the same sounds but different spellings. Yr 2: T. 1

Effective teaching
Use of a familiar text to teach words that rhyme.
Use of stimulating and relevant activities so that children are motivated and learn willingly.
Foster collaborative paired work.

Assessment
Apply their knowledge of rhymes to make up rhymes that have the same spellings and those that do not.

Resources
Nursery Rhyme Big Book, copies of text, magnetic board and letters, Lucky dip box, set of rhyming words, worksheets.

Lesson development
Introduction
Shared read — whole class
Introduce the children to the nursery rhyme 'Humpty Dumpty'.
Encourage them to look.
Question — What can you see?
           What do you think the words are about? Chat.
Remember — The relationship between the words and pictures.
Read the title and the text using the pointer. Keep up the rhythm
allowing children to predict what is coming up next. Repeat the
reading inviting the children to join in.

Focus — rhyming words
Today we are going to learn about words that rhyme.
Question — What are words that rhyme? Chat in pairs.
           Can you tell me the rhyming words? Chat.
On a second copy highlight the pairs that rhyme in different
colours. Let's read them together.
Question — What do you notice about the words? Discuss spelling
           patterns. (15 mins)

Word level
Explain that some words that rhyme do not always have the same
spelling pattern. Find the pairs of rhyming words that have the
same/do not have the same spellings.

Lesson development
We are going to begin our rhyme work by investigating words with
the same spelling patterns.
Develop the **all** rhyme using the magnetic board. Ask children to
think of some **all** words. Let them use the magnetic letters to spell
the words. Teacher to scribe the list of words. Read together.
(15 mins)

Tasks
Teacher to explain each task to each group of children. Some
will be working collaboratively in pairs. Explain the roles of the
teachers. Explain the rules for the task time. Choose a group to
feedback in plenary.

Task 1
Rhyming egg halves (independently)
Children are asked to put together two halves of an egg, each with
a word in. If the words form a rhyming pair, the halves will fit
together. If they don't rhyme they won't fit together. When they
have made their own 'rhyme eggs', they will discover that some

31

have the same spellings at the end of the words and others do not. Make two lists showing this.

Task 2
Rhyming wall (pairs)
The children are given a sheet of bricks in a wall. The first word is written on the first brick of each row. Children have to find other rhyming words which have the same spelling pattern.

Task 3
Help Humpty! (pairs — teacher)
Children are presented with a problem — How can we help Humpty to put him together again?
In their pairs think of some solutions. Discuss as a group, record their own idea in the form of a picture and simple sentence.

Resources
Extra task — Humpty Dumpty worksheet — sequence the nursery rhyme.

Task 4 (pairs — teacher)
The children are given a Lucky Dip Box. Inside the box are 4 key words each for the rhyming families **at** and **en**. They also have two smaller boxes which are labelled **at** and **en**. In their pairs children pull out a picture/word from the box. They then read it using the picture clue, identify the rhyme and place the card inside the appropriate rhyme box.
Extension:
Record the contents of each box. (20 mins)

Plenary — whole class
Group — Rhyming egg halves to feedback. Explain what they did and what they learnt?
Teacher — What have we learnt today?
How have we worked?
Have you enjoyed the tasks? (10 mins)

Case study 3

Enlarged text — *A Necklace of Raindrops* **by Joan Aitken**

Learning outcomes
Sentences cannot make sense without verbs.
Compare a range of story settings.

Use a frame to make simple non-chronological notes using information from a text.

Effective teaching
Teacher questioning to encourage pupils to verbalise thinking.
Pupils to have planned talk time and work to time targets set.
Teacher to model use of writing frame for pupils.
Pupils to use a planning frame to organise thoughts and ideas for writing.

Assessment
Pupils can say that a sentence must have a verb.
Pupils have used the frame successfully to organise thoughts and ideas to write their own ending to the story.

Resources
Big Book: *A Necklace of Raindrops* (Joan Aiken) OHTs of story, OHP Pens, scrap paper, writing frames (and copy on OHT).

Lesson development
Shared read
Look at the cover of the book.
Give the pupils 1 minute to discuss in pairs three things that they notice about the book. Feedback.
Mention author, title, illustrator etc.

Read together until, 'Laura started to cry.'
Read briskly and with pace and intonation.

Talk in pairs about 3 things which have happened in the story so far relating to the titles on the planning frame. Think about: setting, main events, characters and the dilemma which will have to be solved in your story. Put the frame on the OHP to remind the pupils what they will be discussing. 3 minutes.

Discuss the frame and the pupils' ideas. Fill in the Dilemma Box together.

Sentence level work
Look at some of the verbs in the story. Highlight them. Ask the pupils to remind each other what the job of a verb is. Can they tell you what tense it is in?

On a blank OHP sheet. Ask the children to think of some sentences about the story. Write on the OHP. Underline verb. Repeat.

Now ask the pupils to try to think of a sentence which hasn't got a verb. They can go back to their seats for 5 minutes and make their notes on the scrap paper.

Back together, try to find a sentence without a verb. Are there any? What does this tell us about the composition of sentences?

Lesson development
Paired work.
Look together at the writing frame again, remind each other what it is for.
It includes all the areas that were talked about earlier so they should try to remember what was said.

In note form, the pupils fill in the 4 small raindrops. Why do they think they should do this? What do we mean by note form? 1.5 minutes to fill in the first raindrop. One pair to share. Repeat for all four.

Recap the solution or dilemma which must be solved in their ending.

Complete their ending using the notes to help them stay on track and this time they should be using sentences. Everyone should start where the story left off . . . 'Laura started to cry.'

Plenary
2 pairs to join together and share their endings. 1 pair to read first. The other pair must comment on 1 thing which they think is really good about the other pairs' work. Now reverse roles.
Talk about 2 differences in the endings you have just heard.

Back on carpet:
What did we learn about? How did we work together?
Why did we use a writing frame?
What do we know about composing sentences?

Extension: How do different adjectives change the mood of a story? Pupils could change the adjectives in a paragraph and see the effects.

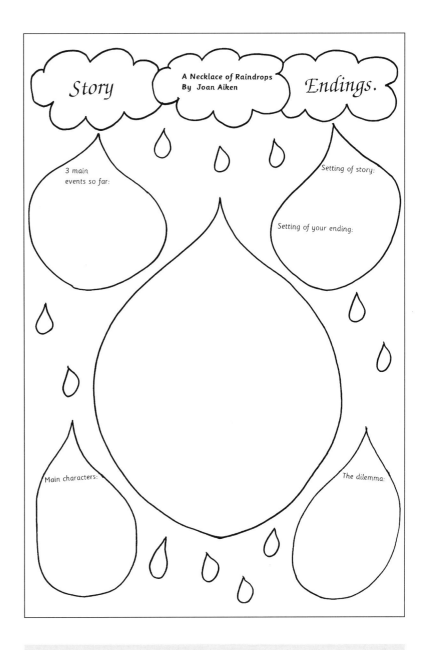

Story — A Necklace of Raindrops By Joan Aiken — Endings.

3 main events so far:

Setting of story:

Setting of your ending:

Main characters:

The dilemma:

Case study 4

Big Book — *The Hungry Giant* by Joy Cowley
Children working collaboratively in the nursery

Learning outcomes
To have experience of a letter writing format.
To compose a shared piece of text.
To make a story prop to use for re-telling the story and for role play.

Effective teaching
Making explicit to children what they are learning and why.
To model writing for a group, showing what writing is and how it is done.
To make the learning experience enjoyable so that the children are motivated.

Resources
The Hungry Giant (Big Book), cardboard boxes, paint, wool, glue, shiny paper, scissors, large sheet, paper, felt tip pen, large envelope

Lesson development
Starting point: Whole class
Shared read of *The Hungry Giant*, taken by the class teacher.

(10 mins)

Main lesson
The children will work in 4 groups. (20–25 mins)

Group 1: Making a mask of the giant's head
Make explicit what the children are going to learn and why.
Show the children the resources available and ask them to think how they might use them to make a mask of the giant's head. Tell the person sitting by you your ideas.
Prompts: What colour will the face be?
  What sort of hair will your giant have?
  How will you make the eyes?
Children may need encouragement in answering the questions.

Children will then be encouraged to work in pairs helping each other to make their mask.
Teacher to intervene, where and when is necessary helping with manipulative skills and asking children to verbalise what they are doing: what colours, materials they are using and how they are using them.

Group 2: Shared writing — letter to the giant
Make explicit to the children what they are doing and why.
They are going to write a letter to the giant to ask him why he is angry.
Show them a prepared example as a model. Discuss the layout:
- the address;
- the starting words;
- the words the letter ends with.

Remind the children of the 'rules' for working together:

- they take turns;
- they help each other;
- they listen carefully to the others in the group.

Ask the children who the letter is being written to, and what words should be used to start the writing.

Then ask them to tell the person sitting by them what they want to ask the giant.

Teacher to scribe as the children say what they want to ask the giant.

When the text is finished, read it through to the group pointing to the words with the pointer.

If any parts need to be changed, ask the children to do so with the teacher scribing.

Teacher then tells the group that she will make a neat copy of the letter to send to the giant.

When the final copy is written show the children the envelope and discuss the address and the need to put a stamp on it.

Ask the children where the letter has to go next. Tell them one of the teachers will post it on their way home tonight.

Activity 3 and 4

3　Read around the room painting and caption writing.
4　Individual writing — What is the giant shouting?
　　Organised by the class teacher.

Plenary

What has each group been doing? Ask children to report back.
What have you learnt?
Praise good ways of working.　　　　　　　　　(10 mins)

Follow up activities

1　Use the giant masks for independent role play and guided story telling.
2　Write a reply from the giant to the letter in the shared write.

Case study 5: lesson I

Big Book — *Mrs Wishy Washy*

Learning outcomes
To have the opportunity to take on the role of a character.
To write independently.

Effective teaching
Children verbalising what they are doing.
Explicit instructions.

Resources
Big Book: *Mrs Wishy Washy*. Scarf, apron; large picture of
Mrs Wishy Washy. Smaller pictures of Mrs Wishy Washy. Pencils,
paper; farm animals, plastic tub or bath; farm templates, paper,
crayons; paint, paper card; tracing cards, pattern cards

Lesson development
Starting point: Whole class
Shared read of *Mrs Wishy Washy* by Joy Cowley.   (10 mins)
What do you think this book is going to be about?
How do you know?
Does anyone know the title?

Read the title page to the class pointing to the words with a
pointer as you read. Read all the book without stopping, pointing
to the words as they are read. Keep up the rhythm of the text
so that the children can predict what is coming next. Encourage
them to join in.
Read for the second time, giving the opportunity for the children to
join in.
Encourage them to take on the voice of the character.
Ask the children to tell the person sitting by them what they would
say to the dirty cow/pig/duck. Share their ideas, encourage them to
use the character's voice.

Developing roles   (5 mins)
Support teacher to take on the role of Mrs Wishy Washy.
Choose 3 children to take on the role of the cow, pig and the duck.
Role play the scene where Mrs Wishy Washy is telling the animals
off for being dirty.
Ask if any of the children would like to take on the role of Mrs
Wishy Washy.
Role play scenes from the story with the children in this role.

Modelling the writing activity   (5 mins)
Support teacher in role of Mrs Wishy Washy.
Ask the children to think and then tell the person sitting by them
what they are going to say to explain how they got dirty.
Share ideas with the class.
Class teacher to share her reason and model how to write it on the
large sheet of paper.
Read the writing together and then show the children the paper
they will be using. Remind them that they should write on their

own and then they can share their work with the teacher who is on their table.

Also tell the children that they can share their writing with the other children at the end of the lesson.

Briefly explain the other activities set out.

Class teacher will allocate the children to their groups.

Children will rotate around the activities.

Activity 1: low guidance
Farm animals and small bath or plastic tub.
Children to role play Mrs Wishy Washy washing the dirty animals.

Activity 2: low guidance
Farm animal templates.
Children to draw around match and then copy the correct animal's name.

Activity 3: with adult
Children paint a scene from the story and write a sentence to be displayed with it. Children to have a try at their own writing and copy their draft onto a suitable piece of card for a label.

Activity 4: low guidance
Children to work at independent writing tasks in the writing area. e.g. Tracing patterns, copy writing, left to right orientation.

Getting on
Children will be encouraged to write on their own. When they have finished their writing they will be asked to read it through to themselves and then read it to the teacher.

The teacher will then scribe the words underneath the child's, explaining that these are the correct spellings and will help all the class to be able to read the writing.

The teacher will then read the writing back to the child to see if they are happy with it. If they are not ask them to change the necessary parts.

Plenary (30 mins — total, not each group)

Ask the children to share their writing with the class.

The other children will be asked to respond positively. 'Tell me some thing you liked about that writing.'

Ask the children to tell the others about the work they have done on the other tables.

Praise any good ways of working.

Ask the children what they would tell Mr Ward about what they have been doing this morning.

What have they learned? (10 mins)

Case study 5: lesson 2

Big Book — *Mrs Wishy Washy*

Learning outcomes
To take on the role of a character.
To write independently.
To use specific vocabulary when talking about books.

Effective teaching
Explicit vocabulary.
Children verbalising what they are doing.

Resources
Big book version of *Mrs Wishy Washy*, vocabulary card-title;
scarf, apron; small sheet of Mrs Wishy Washy; pencils; vocabulary
card-author

Lesson development
Starting point: Whole class
Shared read of *Mrs Wishy Washy*.   (5 mins)
Do you remember this book?
What is the **title**? Using the pointer read the title together.
Who can remember which animals were in the story? Tell the
person sitting next to you. Share this with the class.

Read all the book without stopping pointing to the words with the
pointer as you read. Encourage the children to look at the words
and join in.
Read for the second time, giving the opportunity for the children to
join in.
Encourage them to take on the voice of the characters.

Developing roles   (10 mins)
Refer to the page where Mrs Wishy Washy has cleaned the animals
and goes back into her house.
Support teacher to take on the role of Mrs Wishy Washy.
'I'm glad those dirty animals are clean, now I can get back to the
house and finish what I was doing.'
'I wonder if any of you would like to come and help me in my
house?'
'If you can guess what I was doing you can come and help me.'
(Hopefully some of the children will make some suggestions)
Choose one of the suggestions and get that child to role play the
activity with Mrs Wishy Washy.

Ask if any of the children would now like to take on the role of Mrs Wishy Washy.

Role play what they would be doing in the house.

Modelling the writing activity (5 mins)

Ask the children to tell the person sitting by them what they think Mrs Wishy Washy was doing in her house when she had finished cleaning the animals.

Share their ideas with the class.

Support teacher to model how to write it on the paper the children will be using.

Read the writing together using the pointer.

Tell the children they are going to write their own piece of work and that at the end of the lesson we will read some children's work to the class.

Class teacher will prepare and explain the other activities which are set out and allocate the children to their groups.

Children will rotate around these activities.

Getting on (25 mins total)

Children will be encouraged to write on their own.

When they have finished they will be asked to read their work through to themselves and then read it to the teacher.

The teacher will scribe the words underneath the child's, explaining that these are the correct spellings and will help all the class be able to read the writing.

The teacher will then read the writing back to the child to see if they are happy with it. If they are not then ask them to change the necessary parts.

Plenary

Ask some of the children to share their writing with the class.

(5–10 mins)

Tell me something you liked about that writing.

This morning you have all been an **author**. Has anyone heard this word before?

Explain the meaning and tell the children that their writing is going to be made into a class book.

We will be able to read the book as soon as it is put together.

Look at the work children have done from the other activities, ask them to tell the other children what they have been doing.

What have they learned this morning?

Case study 6

Using a familiar story — *Goldilocks and the Three Bears*

Learning outcomes
Using the language of story in a real context and for real communication.
Opportunity to take on the role of a character.
Developing listening, speaking and writing skills.

Effective teaching
Teacher modelling for the children and providing examples of appropriate responses.
Giving explicit instructions and making the expected outcome clear.
Children working in variety of ways around a common theme.

Assessment
Type of language used for retelling the story.
Competence at individual writing/speaking task.

Resources
Series of line drawings (p. 44), paper, glue, tape recorder and cassette; bear templates, card, wax or large crayons, scissors, sticks, sellotape. Compare bears, writing frame-speech bubble, card, pencils and crayons

Lesson development
Starting point
Taken by the class teacher.   (10 mins)

Development   (40 mins total)
Tell the children that we are going to work in three different groups. Each group will be working on a different activity with a teacher. At the end of the activity we will share what each group has been doing.

Children split into 3 groups by the class teacher.

Group 1
Sequencing the story
Show the children the line drawings and explain that the task is for them to work together to put the pictures into a sequence, in order to retell the story of Goldilocks.
Ask the children to chat and order the drawings and then paste them in the right order onto paper.
They then retell the story as closely to the original text as possible with their partner, using the drawings as prompts.

Record the children's retelling of the story in English and/or home languages.
Play back the tape for the group to listen to and then discuss.
Follow up
Write sentences to match the line drawings.
Put sentences onto language master cards.
Enlarge texts for shared reading.
Make into little books, children illustrating and designing the cover.

Group 2
Making puppets
Tell the group that they are going to make some bear stick puppets.
Ask if anyone can tell us what a puppet is? If not explain to the group.
Children to use the prepared templates of the bears.
Sort the templates into order by size and name the Daddy, Mummy and the Baby bears.
Discuss the appropriate colours to use and then let each child colour their bear.
Children then cut out their bear, with help from the teacher if necessary and attach the stick on the back.
Choose one pair to make a Goldilocks puppet.
When the puppets are made the teacher can then tell the story to the group and through their puppet the children can role play one of the bears or Goldilocks, speaking in the character's voice.
Follow up
Write what the characters say and make into a simple play script.

Group 3
Individual writing
Ask the group to sort the Compare Bears.
Can they find a Mummy Bear, a Daddy Bear and a Baby Bear?
Ask them to stand the bears on the table in a line starting with the Daddy Bear and ending with Baby Bear. Which bear is the biggest? Which bear is the smallest?
Remind children of the part of the story where the bears find Goldilocks in Baby Bear's bed.
Ask the children to hold the right sized bear and take on the role of that bear by speaking in a 'bear' voice saying what that bear would say to Goldilocks.
Teacher to model if responses are limited by taking on the role of the Daddy Bear.
Now we are going to write what the bear says to Goldilocks.
Teacher to model this for the children on the speech bubble frame.
Children then will write individually. The teacher will listen to completed work and scribe any necessary words under the child's writing.

Ask children to share their writing with the group at the end of the activity.

When writing is complete the children can make the remaining story props: 3 bowls, 3 beds, 3 chairs.

Plenary

Taken by the class teacher. (10 mins)

Follow up

The children will now have the necessary story props and puppets to tell the story in different ways.

Set up an area for this in the classroom.

Case study 7

**Example 7: Using *Goldilocks and the Three Bears*
(different activities)**

Learning outcomes
Awareness that print has meaning.
Learning specific book vocabulary.
Opportunity to take on the role of a character.

Effective teaching
Explicit instructions.
Teacher modelling for the children.

Resources
Big Book version of *Goldilocks*, pointer, large sheets of paper; felt
pen; Compare bears, Big story book; Bear templates, wax or large
crayons, sticks, sellotape, laminated large bear, smaller bear
templates

Lesson development
Starting point: Whole class   (10–15 mins)
Shared read of *Goldilocks and the Three Bears*.
What do you think this book is going to be about?
How do you know?
Does anyone know the title? Read the title to the children pointing
to the words with a pointer as you read. Keep the pointer
underneath the text so that the words just read are not covered up.
Ask if anyone has read this story before, if yes tell them that they
will be able to help when we read it together.

Read through the whole book without stopping, pointing to the
words with the pointer as you read. Encourage the children to join
in, especially when the bears are speaking.
Read for a second time, giving the children the opportunity to join
in and speak in role of one of the bears.

Developing the story   (3 mins)
Ask the children to tell you the part of the story they liked. Ask
them to say why they liked this part.
Ask if there was a part of the story they didn't like, ask them to say
why not.
Tell the children we are going to work in groups. Each group will
be working on a different activity with their teacher. At the end of
the activity we will share what each group has been doing.

Children to be split into 4 groups by the class teacher.   (25 mins total)

Group 1

Shared writing

Tell the group that they are going to retell the story of Goldilocks. They will decide what they want to write but the teacher will do the actual writing on the large sheets of paper.

Make sure that all the group are sitting facing the paper.

Suggest some 'rules' for the activity.

e.g. They take turns around the group.

They listen carefully to the others in the group.

They help each other.

Ask who has got a good start for the story and as the children begin to compose the teacher scribes on the large paper. Try to encourage the children to talk to the person next to them about what comes next in the story. When the text is finished, read it through to the group pointing to the words as you read.

Ask if they are happy with all the parts of the story, if not go back and change those parts.

Group 2

Compare Bears

Tell the group that they are going to sort the Compare Bears.

Ask the children if they can find a Mummy Bear, a Daddy Bear and a Baby Bear.

Go round the group 'Tell me the colour of your Mummy Bear.'

Then repeat for the Daddy Bear and Baby Bears.

Ask them to stand the bears on the table in a line starting with the Daddy Bear and ending with Baby Bear. Which bear is the biggest? Which bear is the smallest?

Using the big book read the story to the group again. At the appropriate parts of the story where the bears talk ask the children to hold the right sized bear and take on the role of one of the bears by speaking in a 'bear' voice saying some of the words from that page.

At the end of the story ask the children to sort the Compare Bears into colour sets, children to verbalise the colours as they are sorting.

Group 3

Making puppets

Tell the group that they are going to make some bear stick puppets.

Ask if anyone can tell us what a puppet is? If not explain to the group.

Children to use the prepared templates of the bears.

Sort the templates into order by size and name the Daddy, Mummy and the Baby Bears.

Discuss the appropriate colours to use and then let each child colour their bear.

Children then cut out their bear, with help from the teacher if necessary and attach the stick on the back.

If time allows the teacher can then tell the story to the group and through their puppet the children can role play one of the bears, speaking in the character's voice.

Group 4
Individual writing
Tell the children that they are going to do some writing about the bears.

We are going to write what the bear says to Goldilocks.

Teacher takes on the role of the Daddy Bear.

'Look at my bowl, who's eaten all my porridge?'

Ask some of the children to take on the role of one of the bears, the others listening to what is said.

Teacher will then model the writing on the large bear paper so that the children can see where writing starts, the words and the word spacing.

Children will then be asked to have a try at their own writing on individual bear paper. The children will read their work to the teacher when it is completed and the teacher will write the correct spellings underneath the child's writing.

Tell the children they can share their writing with the rest of the class at the end of the lesson.

Plenary
Ask the children what was the title of the story today?

Then ask each group in turn to show and tell the others what they have been doing.

Praise good ways of working.

Follow up/extension activities
Make a puppet of Goldilocks, and make the other props in the story. Use these to retell the story.

Make the shared writing into a Big Book, illustrated by the children.

Illustrate the shared writing with paintings and make it into a 'Read around the class'.

Make the individual writing into a small book for the book corner.

Using story (Yr 2)
The King's Pudding by Joy Cowley

A writing frame to scaffold children's writing. It can be used with the whole class — step by step instructions.

The King's Pudding

Describe the pudding.

It was
-
-
-

How many puddings did the King make?

Why didn't the King eat his first pudding?

Who stopped the King?	Why?

Describe how the pudding was eaten.
-
-
-
-

What did the King finally do?

Staffroom noticeboards

The curriculum area noticeboards in the staffroom are an excellent vehicle for displaying information about the area being targeted. Try to put up an eye-catching display of the main points about the importance of, for example, 'modelling'. Accompany this with a list of useful texts and articles for reference. For example:

- Modelling enables children to observe, understand and organise their knowledge in order to benefit their own reading and writing.
- Children are able to see how a writer gets started.
- Children are able to see how a writer puzzles over spelling and punctuation.
- The modelled examples are introduced in meaningful contexts therefore the learning becomes embedded.

Suggestion

Produce some handouts with key points, invite written feedback and file it so that eventually it might be possible to produce a small booklet on 'Modelling Reading and Writing at Our School'.

- The teacher has high expectations from the exercise and the children expect to use the knowledge they have gained.
- Once the children have made the connections between the modelling and how they can use the knowledge, engagement has taken place and they are fully involved in their own learning.

At this point it is almost possible to hear the reader groaning and saying 'But I haven't got time to do all this'. Time management is definitely the next issue to attack.

Time

If you are not careful you will be run off your feet trying to be everything to everyone at once and you will achieve very little. You must not spread yourself too thinly. As you probably have a class to teach as well as your role as coordinator then you need to have a timetable of availability. This timetable has to suit you and the way you work. Some teachers like to stay late after school to plan and prepare for the next day. Others might abandon that because a really good idea has struck on the drive home so you end up rushing in the next morning to change everything. Some prefer to get to school early to sort out the day. A stream of afternoon planners popping in for a chat, asking for equipment or needing reassurance is not what most coordinators need. You might decide to invite colleagues to discuss issues after school and set aside one afternoon a week for extended consultation time.

It is also a good idea to suggest that highly contentious issues are not raised at times of brief respite, i.e. when you are trying to catch a quick cup of coffee at playtime. You certainly don't want to be attacked by someone fired up about the spelling policy and demanding instant action. Of course it is to be hoped that feelings would not get to that level, but everyone who has been in schools for a while will recognise the scenario. At such times a deathly hush descends on the normally vibrant room and you are faced with an audience to see how you deal with the situation. Don't be drawn in, suggest a quiet word at 4 pm. Dealing with people in a very public place when they are wound up and you are unprepared is definitely not a good idea.

Similarly with parents: if the parents are prone to popping in for a chat, then encourage them to come in the afternoon. Examples exist where parents are welcome to tiptoe into the classroom at storytime at the end of the day twice a week. It is really lovely to see parents engrossed in the stories and sharing the pleasure with their young children, whilst at the same time learning so much about the skill of sharing texts with young learners and developing a deeper awareness of the books children enjoy. At home time they then saw anything of particular interest that their child wanted to share and could have a word or two and get worries voiced before they came to explosive crisis point. We will return to this later when we talk about parental involvement.

Apart from a day-to-day awareness of time you also need to look at the medium and long term and work out the timing for involvement in staff development. Before you get heavily involved though, you need to spend a fair amount of time deepening your own knowledge of the subject. See if there are any courses being run that would help with this and might also get you involved in discussion with other English coordinators. One enormous advantage of attending a good course is that you have the chance to observe the presentation skills of the course leaders. Make a note of the techniques they use. Watch the way they group people and move them around. A really good course will teach you so much more than just the content knowledge.

Sharing the curriculum initiative

With the children

Often when we talk with children about their learning and things that happen regularly in classrooms we ask, 'Why do you think you do that?' Some of the answers come as a real surprise to teachers.

'I don't know, because Miss says we have to.'
'We just do it, that's what you do on Monday morning.'

Children, even very young ones of 5 and 6, are quite capable of being told and understanding the reason why we do things in school. Encourage the teachers to talk to the children about learning. Tell them to explain to the children that we have got new easels to use on the carpet so that when we are sharing a Big Book everyone can see it clearly and their teacher has two hands free to point to words and pictures to help them to understand about how reading works. Tell them to talk to the children about how reading happens for different people at different times, but that it usually happens for everyone sooner rather than later. Talk about the reasons for sitting down together and talking about how people spend time and what has been happening to them. Talk to them about why 'circle time' is important. Tell the children that it is to help them to learn how to listen carefully and speak clearly. Tell them that when you write about the events on the large sheets of paper on the easel it is to help them to learn about how writing works and then we all read it and it helps us to learn to read too. It is just possible that sometimes we underestimate the powers of understanding of these young learners. Whatever the circumstances, or environment of the school, it is vitally important to hold high expectations of what can be achieved. If you expect a lot from the children and involve them in their own learning then you will reap the benefits.

Case study

Example 1: Being explicit with children

Learning outcomes
Experience of using pictures to structure a story.
Working interactively in a group to produce a piece of writing.

Effective teaching
Children working collaboratively in a group.
Giving clear objectives at the start of the lesson and reviewing learning at the end.
Making learning an enjoyable experience.

Resources
4 pictures, paper, pencils and pens

Lesson Development
Starting point: Whole class   (10–15 mins)
Support teacher
Make the task explicit to the class: they are going to write a story, working together in a group.

Recall learning from the previous lesson on the structure of a story. Remind children if necessary, that stories have a start, a middle and an ending.

Show children the four pictures that are being used for today's story. Chat in pairs about the pictures:

- What can you see?
- Who are the characters (people and animals in this story?)
- Discuss key vocabulary with the children: dog, toy-box, girl, soldier (man, boy)
- What else do you want to know?

Development: Group work (support teacher, class teacher and NNEB) Children working in three groups   (30 mins total)
Remind children of the rules for working collaboratively.
Look at the pictures again. Ask the children to talk to their partner about the order they think the pictures should be in.
Sequence the pictures in the correct order with the children verbalising the key events. Make explicit the parts of this story i.e. Which is the beginning the middle and the ending.
Give each pair of children one picture and tell them that their task is to write the text for that part of the story. Make explicit that they must only write about the events in their picture and then we will put the writing together to make our story.
All the group will help to write the ending.
When each piece of text is finished the children will read it to the teacher who will scribe the correct spellings underneath if necessary.
Read the text with the children and check that the parts fit together, work with the children to make any changes.
All the group will then make suggestions for the ending of the story. This can be written interactively.
Read the whole story with the group and ask them:

- What do you like about your story?
- Do you want to change any parts? Why and how? Make any further changes to the text at this point and read it through again.

Children can then colour in the illustrations and with the teacher's help make the work into a book for the classroom.

Plenary: Whole class   (10–15 mins)
Taken by the class teacher.

Case study

Example 2: Being explicit with children

Learning outcomes
Experience of structuring a story, with a start, middle and an ending.
Working collaboratively to produce a piece of writing.

Effective teaching
Teacher modelling the reading and writing activity.
Working on a collaborative task.
Explicit instructions and clear objectives given at the start of the
task.

Resources
Buster McCluster story; A3 paper, pencils, crayons, card, felt tip
pens

Lesson development
Starting point
Shared read of *Buster McCluster*.
What do you think this book is going to be about?
How do you know?
Does anyone know the title?

Read the title page to the class pointing to the words with a pointer
as you read. Read all of the book without stopping, pointing to the
words as they are read. Keep up the rhythm of the text so that the
children can predict what is coming next. Encourage them to join in.

Second read:
Read again, stop to look at the pictures. Discuss, picking out key
vocabulary.
Focus on the structure of the story:
Make explicit to the children that stories have a start, a middle,
and an ending.
Bring out the parts of this story by asking questions:
- What did Buster do first?
- When the sprouts grew what happened while Buster was
  sleeping?
- How did the story end?
Ask children to tell their partner what happened and then share
each idea with the class.

Development   (35 mins total)
Tell the children that they are going to be working collaboratively
in a group.

You will be talking to each other about the story so you must remember the rules.

Take turns

Be sensible

Listen carefully to what the other person is saying

Don't interrupt

Share the work

Make the task explicit to the children: to retell in writing the story of Buster.

Ask the children to pick out the key events from the story.
Digging, planting, growing, bugs and slugs coming, cooking and exploding.
Teacher to scribe these on separate pieces of card and then put them in sequence with the group.
Start with the first key word 'digging'. Ask the group to think how we could start the story. What could they write? Tell the person next to you what you are going to say.
Share ideas — teacher to model the writing on the first sheet of paper.
Read this together, then repeat for the next key word. Each time read all of the previous text so that the children are aware of the story building up.
Encourage children to be interactive with the writing.
Children may combine the middle events so that the story is in less than seven parts.
Before writing the final page remind the group that this is the ending of the story.
When the text is finished read it through to the group pointing to the words as you read.
Re-read and discuss any changes that may need to be made.
Children can then illustrate each page of the story, individually or in pairs.

Plenary (10 mins)

Read each story even if illustrations are unfinished.
Ask children to listen for how each group has structured their story.
What did you like about the writing?
Would you change anything — why and how?
What have you learned?

Follow up

Make each group's story into a book for the classroom.

Children to retell a familiar story using a series of cartoon pictures.
Work in pairs or with an adult to produce the writing.

Suggestion

Some English coordinators hold a regular 'Reading hour' say, on the first Monday of each month from 3.30–4.30, so that parents can come in and sit down with a cup of tea and discuss the reading process in a relaxed atmosphere. What develops is a group support situation when a mother can say something like, 'my daughter doesn't want to read to me she wants to be read to,' and another can chip in with, 'oh yes, my son used to do that, it just lasted a week or so and then he was happy to read again.' Often all parents want is a bit of reassurance backed up with specific knowledge when required. If this takes place in the school library then the children can be looking at books whilst the parents chat.

Tell the parents

It's a good idea to keep parents informed of changes in your curriculum area. This can be done at a curriculum evening when parents are invited into school to hear about aims for the coming term or year. Often this is done in the form of a newsletter. However you decide to do it, keeping parents informed of changes that affect their children is in the best interest of everyone.

Probably the area of greatest concern when children start school is 'when will my child read?' A 'Reading Evening' once a year to explain the school's approach to the teaching of reading will inform, give confidence, help to alleviate worries and go some way to encouraging the sharing of books with children in the home.

Good parental relationships can be an advantage in many ways. One idea for building up the school library is to invite new children and their parents to buy a book at discounted price to donate to the library. This book would then have an inscription inside it with the child's name and the date of the donation. The books have previously been selected and bought from the English budget and parents and children are asked to choose from this selection. The money raised from this sale is ploughed back into the book buying fund. Organising a budget and spending that money wisely is another facet of the coordinators' role.

The English budget

In some schools each curriculum area is given a certain, equal amount of money each year to spend on new resources and equipment. However in most schools coordinators might be asked to put in a bid for a share of the available money. This is often further controlled by the priorities established within the School Development Plan which is reviewed and revised on an annual basis. Whatever the system, careful planning and budgeting is necessary.

Where a major initiative in English is taking place it might be necessary for the coordinator to plan expenditure over a number of years. For example the purchase and covering of Big Books. These are an expensive item and they need to have their life expectancy prolonged for as long as possible by covering in plastic and careful storage, possibly on purpose made racks. Books would seem to be the number one priority in the English department of a school. You might be building up a stock of multiple copies of books that motivate children at different stages of the reading process. Perhaps you have agreed as a staff to stock a new reading scheme. Decisions need to be made in collaboration with colleagues and all this has to fit into a time frame. We are all no doubt familiar with the panic to get your hands on the educational catalogues a few weeks before the deadline for requisitions but a clear strategy is better and avoids mistakes and duplication.

Decisions will have to be made as to whether people have an individual allowance for special items that are theirs to use, but not *ad infinitum.*

Budget planning is often the forerunner of a new curriculum initiative because it is no good introducing a new idea, firing everyone up with enthusiasm and then watching it all fade because you cannot resource the project properly.

As we reach the end of this first section, the enormity of the role is unravelling. It is a big job, but with adequate foundation work, a buoyant personality, strong commitment, a good sense of humour and the ability to listen to the messages that people are giving you, albeit in roundabout ways, you should survive with a smile on your face and hopefully be enjoying the challenge.

Chapter 3

Strategies for staff development

Organising Inset

Anything you are planning to do in the way of staff development needs to be discussed with the senior management team so that it fits within the school's development planning.

Bringing in a course leader

You will need to decide whether you are going to lead the in-service sessions yourself, or whether you are going to invite an experienced course leader to work with the staff. Funding will probably determine the possibility of the latter, but it is worth bearing in mind, as an outsider can get straight down to the nitty gritty of the situation and can tease out issues that you might not have the confidence to broach. You could then plan follow-up sessions that you would lead yourself. If it is a big initiative then this is a good idea, if not you might prefer to save this option for later and plan by yourself. The advantages for an external input are:

- You will probably be allocated a staff development day which is infinitely preferable to a curriculum session at the end of a busy school day.

- You will have an experienced course leader skilled at developing the thinking of groups of teachers.

Suggestion

Introduce a new idea and then invite a teacher from a school that has already developed the curricular area that you are moving towards to come and talk to your colleagues. Alternatively, you could arrange visits for colleagues to see the approach in action. Whatever you decide, some input will be necessary first.

- They will have all the material prepared.

- They will be giving messages that everyone will hear at first hand.

- Objections and worries can be dealt with by someone outside the school who is used to dealing with conflict.

Naturally, costing is an issue but schools do have funding for staff training and most now plan spending in this area as part of a Curriculum Development Plan. Alternatives include the local support services, e.g. advisers, advisory teachers, curriculum development centre staff or your local university school of education – all could be approached to talk to staff about current issues in curriculum development.

Leading Inset yourself

The most important issues to sort out are when and where. So many internal Inset sessions occur after a 'brief' staff meeting. This is not the time to approach curriculum change. What you need is a specially timetabled occasion that is a stand-alone exercise. So many of us can recall incidents when a coordinator has carefully planned an Inset session, negotiated exclusive time, only to have the headteacher take five minutes to share something important with the staff at the beginning. This 'something of importance' can be devastating news about a family within the school that upsets everyone. How can you follow that? Well the answer is, you can't. It just isn't fair on anyone.

It is a good idea to have an agreed time limit for all meetings, curriculum sessions are no different. There is only so long that tired teachers can be expected to concentrate at the end of a busy day. An hour is a good span but some schools do work for periods of up to three hours and claim it as half a day from their allotted five throughout the year.

You also need to have time to prepare the venue and yourself. Don't go straight from the classroom and the trials of the end of a busy 'infant' day straight into a different role. Ask for at least an hour before the start of the session to prepare. Cover will have to be arranged; it may be difficult and inconvenient but it will be of great benefit. Then think about the venue, this is very important.

Don't attempt to do an Inset session in the staffroom

Don't even contemplate using the staffroom.

- At four o'clock in the afternoon an easy chair is the place where people relax and snooze.

- Staffroom furniture is impossible to rearrange. It is bulky and cumbersome.

- It is a room where people wander around, making a cup of tea, reading the paper, chatting to friends, it does not have the right atmosphere.

- A meeting in the staffroom has no sense of urgency, people are used to wandering in, you will never get everyone there on time.

- You will probably need to use an OHP and this will cause problems. Where would the screen go? How can you ensure that everyone can see? If they can't see they might not pay attention.

- It is very hard to find a focal point in a staffroom where you can stand and talk to the group.

Where else is there?

The hall would be a better place, but don't forget to check that it is not being used for Cubs, Brownies, country dancing or a keep fit class. Assuming that you have access to the hall towards the end of the afternoon then you can decide on the orientation and arrange the seating to your liking.

When deciding on the orientation it will probably be determined by the plug for the OHP and the screen, but as a rule try to avoid standing with your back to the windows. It's not a good background for an audience to focus on you. Also they might become engrossed in the football practice going on outside.

Arrange the seating and give some thought to how you want them to sit: in rows, a small circle, groups of four? The chances are that if you arrange the seating in groups the first people to arrive will straighten the rows up anyway, we teachers are tidy people, so perhaps you could begin in rows and move them swiftly into groups.

Your own classroom is another option, especially if your school is small and we are only talking about a small group. Using different people's classrooms is a good way for everyone to get about the school and see what is going on. It is also a great incentive to teachers to straighten up and change the wall displays. The chairs might be a bit small, but you could bring some others in.

Check the equipment

A small point, but make sure that the equipment is functioning properly and that you know how to use the remote control on the video etc. You want to be sure that everything goes as smoothly as possible.

Overheads

Spend time producing clear, error free overheads. If you are a bit nervous then bullet pointed overheads will keep you going smoothly through your presentation. There are a few dos and don'ts with the use of overheads:

■ Get them all arranged in order before you start, if necessary colour code them for different stages of your presentation.

■ Beforehand, decide which side of the projector you will stand.

■ Don't block people's view of the screen.

■ Don't read aloud what is clearly visible for all to see.

■ Practise placing the overhead so that the top part is visible.

■ As you move from overhead to overhead, decide beforehand where you are going to place the ones you have used in a neat pile, in case you want to return to one later.

■ Make sure you don't trip over the cord. Be aware of where it is, or tape it down, or even place a piece of furniture over it. It is not easy to recover from farcical situations.

Presentation skills

It is only natural to feel nervous, especially if you have never done a presentation before or it is the first one in a new school, or both.

■ Start on time and finish on time. Let it be known that there will be a prompt start. It is so aggravating to arrive on time and then to sit around for ten minutes waiting for late comers. Start the way you intend to continue.

■ Be sure you know what you are talking about.

■ If you are nervous then commit to heart your opening statement. Start well.

■ Smile.

■ Make sure that you make eye contact with everyone in the room during that opening statement. It establishes your control.

■ Appear confident even if you don't feel it, there is nothing more embarrassing for an audience than someone apologising for their inadequacies before they have displayed any.

■ Try not to 'umm' and 'aah' too much. If you are not used to speaking fluently for long stretches then practise, a commentary spoken aloud of your drive to school, or whilst you are preparing a meal, etc. Observers will think you are talking to yourself and going nuts, but that doesn't matter.

■ Empty your pockets of small change, keys, bus tickets and anything you might fiddle with.

■ Decide before you start whether you want to take questions during your presentation or at the end, or at regular intervals during the hour. You decide and tell everyone how it is to be.

■ Have a word with the school secretary who is an ally because you have spent time fostering good relations. Ask her not to interrupt with phone messages but to screen them for urgency.

- End well. Sum up, thank everyone for coming and for being so attentive and responsive.
- Ask for volunteers to help you tidy up.

Remember that the best speakers have had lots and lots of practice. Nobody expects you to make a faultless performance on your first attempt. If there is someone on the staff who appears to present effortlessly, talk to them. You will probably find they were as nervous as you when they first started.

It will probably be decided at the end of your session that further meetings will be needed. These will also have to be well prepared.

Learning to manage meetings

Schools are very busy places and teachers have many demands put upon them. Meetings have to be seen to be necessary and attendance by all involved parties is essential. Meetings are the chance for people to communicate their feelings and be involved in the development of policies. Participation is vitally important because people who have been actively involved in all the stages of a curriculum change are more likely to support and carry it through. It is therefore important for the curriculum leader to become a skilled leader of meetings.

Teachers need to be clear about the purpose of the meeting so that they can prepare to contribute.
- Give everyone an agenda well in advance and if the meeting is only for a small group, post a copy on the noticeboard so that everyone knows what is going on. Rumours about 'secret meetings' can cause no end of unnecessary strife.
- Decide on a venue and a time with starting and finishing times clearly stated.
- Try to arrange for tea and coffee to be available so that people don't get sidetracked when they pop into the staffroom to pick up a drink. A small investment in some biscuits or a cake is often money or effort well spent.
- Be aware of staffroom discussions before the meeting. If this is an issue where feelings run high then it is better to be ready to deal with possible situations of conflict.

Dealing with conflict

Let us return to the example of the adoption of 'modelling' easels in all Key Stage 1 classrooms. You know that the majority of the staff are willing to give it a try. What will you do if someone throws a real wobbler and refuses to comply, saying that you have no right to tell people *how* they are to teach, only what?

Do you feel confident that your headteacher will back you in such a situation or will they back down under the confrontational stand of a difficult but capable member of staff? Is consistency of approach a key thread running through all curriculum areas or just a vision for your own area? This is an issue that has to be addressed because many a good initiative has fallen by the wayside as a result of the headteacher not sharing the full vision of the curriculum coordinator. Perhaps the pace of the change has been too fast. Perhaps a longer trial time was necessary.

Teachers have to see that there was a need for change. Often those who are most resistant are very good at the job they do, but they have got entrenched in their ways and their teaching has not progressed. They often need more time to observe and adapt. There could however be deeper reasons for resistance. Hidden resentment towards you or the headteacher could result in your curriculum initiative being used as the vehicle of dissent.

You need to avoid such a situation taking place. This is where time spent earlier in developing good relationships of trust and genuine concern will hold you in good stead. Coordinators need good inter-personal skills. They have to be able to listen to teachers' concerns and worries and react in a positive, supportive way. They also have to be strong and brave enough to stand up to bullying from time to time. Teachers are used to being in control, they are powerful people and 'face loss' is something hard to handle. You often find that someone will dig themselves into a hole and it is impossible for them to climb out. You have to try to find a satisfactory compromise so that the initiative doesn't falter by losing consistency and a good teacher is not alienated through the mishandling of a meeting.

Suggestion

The success of the innovation will be revealed in what happens in classrooms and that is the bottom line.

Emphasis on the benefits for the children and the success of the school is the best strategy. The acceptance of a move brought about by genuine concern, consultation with staff and collaborative planning will usually result in the individual not wanting to be out on a limb. Everyone needs to feel ownership of the innovation and shared responsibility for a successful outcome.

Working with others

As a coordinator it is important to remember that your role is to aim to make a difference in not only your practical classroom teaching but also to have an impact on others. Therefore there are some key points to bear in mind when working and communicating with others:

- help teachers to realise needs;
- identify focus areas to work on together;
- develop own classroom practice that is informed by analysing how children learn;
- work alongside teachers in the classroom;
- talk about teaching and why you do it the way that you do;
- develop links inside and outside school . . . senior management team, headteacher, other schools and agencies; and
- displays of work around school.

Communicating with others

Asking for support:

- What I value from you.
- What I would appreciate.
- A way in which you could help me now.
- I don't understand why.
- I'm not sure what you are saying — can you clarify it for me?
- I'd like to observe.
- It would help me understand a little more about the situation.

Giving support:

- Could you think how you might . . . ?
- How might we move forward on this?

- Can we talk about how we might move forward?
- So what you are saying is, can I make it clear . . . ?
- Can you think of a way in which you may get involved?
- This is clearly an issue which is of importance to you — what do you think?
- How can we change it to make it right for you?
- Children will benefit if . . .

Part two

What you need to know about English and literacy at KS 1

Chapter 4
Establishing basic beliefs about literacy

Chapter 5
How does all this fit within the Literacy Framework?

Chapter 4   Establishing basic beliefs about literacy

In the light of the government's Literacy Strategy, a deeper knowledge of the reading and writing processes and the way they should be taught is a central focus within schools. To give a greater sense of ownership within each school, staff should develop a set of basic beliefs about literacy in order to ensure that the ways it is taught in the Literacy Framework complement other aspects of the teaching of English within the school.

Basic beliefs

It is important that, as a school, you sit down and agree on your basic beliefs about the acquisition of speaking and listening, reading and writing. The National Curriculum guidelines set an expectation nationally, but the school needs to think of the specific requirements of its own situation. The Literacy Framework goes further and sets the expectation for the specific teaching of literacy on a term-by-term basis. By focusing your attention together on things that are really important for the children you teach, there is more chance that the product will remain in your consciousness. Don't just adopt the beliefs of others, create your own. This gives ownership.

This is an example of one school's beliefs about literacy learning and teaching which were developed by the staff under the management of the coordinator.

- The foundations of literacy are laid at home in the early years.
- We can build on those early foundations to bring the children from oracy into literacy.
- The children need a school that is a language rich environment.
- All reading and writing experiences should be child centred, purposeful and meaningful.
- Literacy learning must always be rewarding because success encourages further reading and writing.
- Through language children explore their world and their views of it. Speaking and listening, reading and writing are therefore inseparable from each other and also from all learning processes.
- As teachers we have a responsibility to make these experiences so stimulating and so rewarding that we produce articulate speakers, concentrated listeners, avid readers and children who enjoy writing.

This then is a philosophy and to bring it about the English coordinator requires knowledge of the learning processes involved, the subject knowledge required and careful planning of how this is all to be taught in each year band within the key stage.

As trained teachers we all have knowledge of the developing learner and an awareness that our teaching must match and extend the developmental stage of the child. We tend to get weighed down in debates about 'methods', especially in the teaching of reading, but often when effective teaching is analysed, the 'method' used is of less significance than teachers' awareness of the process and the needs of individual learners. The Bullock Report highlighted this way back in 1975.

> the difference between good and bad reading teachers is usually not to do with their allegiance to some particular method, but to do with their relationships with children and their sensitivity in matching what they do to each individual child's learning needs.

What is needed is not a superficial knowledge about this method or that, but a deep understanding of the processes involved in acquiring literacy skills. The Literacy Framework acknowledges the problem of the half understood methods, the limited levels of debate and the fluctuation in the use of different methods. It sets out to use all available methods within the context of literacy teaching and applying them to each term of the primary phase. The Key Stage 1 English coordinator is in at the beginning of this process for the school-aged child. It would be a good development if *all* English coordinators began with a time working at Key Stage 1 because it is vitally important to understand the whole story and not to come in halfway through. In the middle and upper primary classes there will unfortunately be some children who are still functioning at a lower level of attainment. An understanding of their learning needs is essential.

Absolute honesty is needed in this sensitive area of teacher knowledge. If we apply for a post as coordinator, then a level of subject knowledge will be expected. However, what often happens is that someone already on the staff is asked to take on the role because their classroom practice is good. This does not necessarily mean that they have been keeping abreast of recent research. Neither does it mean that they have a very deep theoretical knowledge; it could be that they have developed strategies through trial and error that work for them. They are very likely good practitioners. They have developed good methods, but more is needed for this coordination role in which you influence the professional development of your colleagues and inform parents about what you are doing and why you are doing it.

Don't panic, many excellent coordinators began from this point. To study from a strong foundation of good practice across the curriculum and success as a teacher is not a bad place to start! It also heightens the self esteem because you will find yourself frequently muttering, 'of course, we all know that' . . . but do we? Good, informed, instinctive teachers often assume that every member of the profession shares their own insights and visions; realising that they don't can come as a bit of a shock. As you read this section of the book, you will be able to call to mind examples of individual children you have worked with who fit the children being described. It is a tremendous confidence booster and makes for relatively easy learning because the learning is embedded in interest and experience.

To make this as practical and useful as possible, let us look at the theoretical underpinning of the key statements in the list of beliefs that were mentioned at the beginning of this section. What follows is just a taste, an appetiser, but it is a starting point in what otherwise can seem a daunting task.

Key Statement 1: The foundations of literacy are laid at home in the early years

The children

Children have acquired much knowledge before they begin formal schooling. Their acquisition of speech and their knowledge of the meaning and use of around two thousand words in their mother tongue, and for some children in an additional language also, means that they come to school with a great deal of knowledge to build upon.

The degree of support in this learning process will have varied from family to family. When Margaret Clark (1976) was investigating her 'Young Fluent Readers' she found that they all had a rich experience of help in a casual, rather than formal way which was a normal part of the daily life of the family. Parents didn't set aside time to 'teach' their children to read in the heavily structured way that they probably learnt, but instead they simply included their children in literary activities. When Mum wrote a shopping list, so did the child. When Dad wrote a letter to his mother, so did the child, albeit a page of squiggly lines. Parents talked to their children about what they were reading, would show a child a recipe in a book when making a cake, would go to the newspaper to find the time of a favourite TV programme. Children picked up the message that literacy was useful. It was also found that these children were read to regularly. Children who read early have been helped to become aware of print. They will have helped to search for cereal packets on the supermarket shelves because they recognise the colour and shape of the writing on the packet. They build up a sight knowledge of words. One of the first things a teacher needs to do when the children first come into school is to exploit this knowledge and concentrate on the teaching potential of environmental print.

The method

In one school, the English coordinator suggested that the reception class children should make a huge wall display of their favourite breakfast food by collecting boxes and wrappings. The children took delight in 'reading' the names of the cereal packets they recognised. They then made their own personal books by sticking their favourites in a book and the teacher wrote, 'I like . . .' and the children cut out the words from the box and stuck them on the page. The children could all read their own books fluently because the words were in a highly recognisable context. When the teacher wrote, 'I like corn flakes' with a computer font, very few of these children could read the text. The children were able to recognise the visual picture of the word in its context rather than the arrangement of letters. The next stage would therefore be to insert a page into the book with a picture of 'corn flakes' but the printed word placed underneath, to help the children make the connection. Throughout the project the English coordinator was there to encourage, help and above all celebrate the success with the teacher and the children. In a subsequent staff meeting she was able to encourage all staff members to go and look at the excellent work done by the reception class and to point out the learning processes involved. Often displays of this kind are only seen as colourful interior design, the full educational significance needs to be spelled out. Margaret Donaldson (1978) refers to such young children teaching themselves to read largely through their 'encounters with this kind of "public print" '.

Young children have favourite stories that they know by heart. These are often read to them every night at bedtime. Sometimes the reader will try to skip a page to save time but the child soon notices and insists on the full text being read. These much loved books can be the child's way into reading. The words having been committed to heart, connections within the child's observation of the printed words can often trigger the engagement that makes reading possible. The Key Stage 1 English coordinator needs to encourage parents to continue the reading of these favourites as their child begins to be more aware of print. Sartre reportedly taught himself to read by giving himself what he called 'private lessons'. He took a book which his mother had read to him many times and because he knew the text, was able to work out how to read it for himself. It involved persistence, practice and pleasure.

Alan Bennett in his book *Writing Home* refers to his early reading experiences as a very young child,

> *I had read a few story books by this time, as I had learned to read quite early by dint, it seemed to me, of staring over my brother's shoulder at the comic he was reading until suddenly it made sense.*

When you, the English coordinator, are talking to parents about the reading process, do encourage them to think back to their own early learning experiences. It can be quite illuminating. You will undoubtedly find that the parents who get most anxious about the progress of their child were strugglers themselves and don't want their own children to suffer the same frustrations that they experienced. Similarly adults for whom learning to read held no problems can become frustrated with their child who needs more time and help.

Those who are able to reflect usually recall a desire to make sense of print. There was a definite purpose, a need and that need often sprang from a pleasure in hearing and sharing stories in the home and a desire to be able to do it themselves so that the world of books was available at any time, not just at the whim of an elder sibling or a busy parent.

Margaret Meek (1988) discusses the 'reader-like' qualities young children have and suggests that many early reading skills can be missed by teachers if their training has been strictly geared towards 'schooling' literacy. Children have to be given the opportunity to demonstrate what they can already do. Unless they are given the chance to do this the teacher will never be aware of what they already know. As English coordinator you have to encourage your team of teachers to exploit the knowledge the children already have and help them to find interesting ways to build on that understanding.

The teacher

Talking to children about how they became readers can be fascinating. This sobering dialogue with a reflective 10-year-old is a real thought provoker.

Laura: I learnt to read with my mummy before I went to school. We used to read the *Spot* books and I somehow worked out how to read them by myself.

Teacher: What happened when you went to school?

Laura: There weren't any Spot books in the classroom. We all had to sit down and learn the letters.

Teacher: Did you understand why you were doing that?

Laura: No, because when I went home I was just reading more and more books with Mummy and by myself.

Teacher: When were you given a book to read?

Laura: Well, when we had done all the letter sounds we were given words to learn, and when we knew all the words we were given a book.

Teacher: Did you enjoy the book?

Laura: Not really, it wasn't really about anything, it was just for learning to read.

Teacher: Then what happened?

Laura: We moved house and I went to another school.

Teacher: Did you tell the teacher there that you could read?

Laura: Yes, but they did it differently there, we all had to learn to read sentences, and when we could read all the sentences we were allowed to read the page in the book.

Teacher: But Laura, you could read.

Laura: I know, I was reading Fat Puss books at home then. It got better when I was allowed to take a book home, but I was only allowed to read a few pages each day.

Laura lived completely different 'reading lives' at home and at school, because no one found out what she could do. Even if they had, she might not have fitted into the 'method'. They were locked into a 'schooling' approach to literacy learning. Why didn't the teachers realise that she was a reader? Well, maybe they genuinely didn't know. Children are very trusting and accepting of the way they are treated, they fit into systems, they conform, they keep quiet. This is where the gifted child often slips through the net. Another child who heard this conversation was appalled. His recollection was, 'That it just happened in my first year at school.' It didn't actually 'happen' until well into his second year, when all the input from the first year bore fruit, but who's counting time. What is important in his comment is that it shows that the child was aware that becoming a reader was a natural process. It is known that he had a lot of very directed teaching, but it was an integrated part of the whole learning experience of his days at school. What appeared very natural to him was in fact a very structured, informed route to literacy in a rich environment, encompassing many excellent texts that make reading possible. Criticism based on such comments as 'It just happened', have been hurled unjustly at the 'Whole Language' movement especially in the USA, Canada and Australia. In one study, undergraduates interviewed about the way they were taught were unable to recall the processes that they undoubtedly experienced. They just had recollections of the naturalness of it all. Good 'Whole Language' teaching is, if anything, more structured than more traditional approaches which rely on the child reading one publisher prescribed text after another. When children supplement this with a large number of good non-scheme books then the teacher has to plan a reading route through the books for individual children. Perhaps we need to talk to the children more about what we are asking them to do and why they are doing it, making the learning explicit rather than implicit and perhaps 'hidden'. The English coordinator who is able to pop into classrooms on a regular basis is able to talk to the children about this 'reading business'. It's not just the parents who need to understand but also the children.

The nearest example I have ever got of a child being aware of reading actually 'happening', was a 6-year-old girl, who had just become a reader, coming to me in distress and saying, 'This reading thing is scary'. I was astounded. 'Why?', I asked. 'Because I have been trying so hard for you and Mummy for a long time and now I can read without having to do anything, I just have to look and I know what it says.' Scary indeed.

Throughout this book we seem to be saying to the English coordinator, 'Talk to the children'. Observe the children, see how they learn and back this up with your theoretical knowledge about the development of learning. This way you become more and more informed so that when you introduce a topic on, for example, environmental print with the reception class teachers, you can explain *why* it is important to do it.

Key Statement 2: We can build on those early foundations

The children

Young children are great talkers. They love to use words, they love to hear themselves speak, unfortunately they are not so good at listening. In school the ability to listen is going to help them to learn. As the English coordinator you need to be able to be sure that all staff understand and plan for this aspect.

Children need to know:
- when to listen and when to talk;
- how to ask questions;
- how to discuss; and
- how to organise themselves.

In a large group:
- how to pick out the main points, for example, 'I have to put my work away, go and get my PE kit without running, get changed and then sit on the carpet';
- how to focus; and
- how to develop concentration, not an easy thing to do for some 5-year-olds.

In a small group:
- how to help the speaker;
- being ready to join in if needed;
- letting others talk; and
- being aware that listening is not waiting to talk.

The natural desire of young children to talk needs to be channelled into ways to help them learn. They need to work together, to collaborate, to share knowledge and understandings. This is where the classic sentence of Vygotsky (1962) makes its impact:

What the child can do today in cooperation, tomorrow he will be able to do on his own.

Vygotsky's observations led him to see learning as a process of social interactions. What tends to happen in classrooms is that children learn to be quiet. They soon learn to become teacher pleasers, anything for an easy life. The message somehow gets across that the quiet child is the good child. Yes, there are times when they must be quiet, but in so many classrooms the teacher talks far too much of the time. Even young children of 5 and 6 can work together to solve a task. BUT, it has to be about something of importance to the children.

The method

Here is an example of the efforts of a class of 6-year-olds engaged in working in groups of four to try to organise a school assembly in a hurry. There was urgency about the task, the children could see that they needed to be involved to help their teacher otherwise it would not take place. They talked, shared knowledge, suggestions etc. and then struggled together to write it all down with all the sharing that involved.

Here were a group of young children using 'talking and listening' to learn. They all worked very hard. We have to make children value productive, collaborative talk as work and be able to go home and say, 'We worked really hard today at talking.' They 'really worked hard today' at writing too. Look closely at how they wrote. Example 1, the child who wrote this has visual pictures of words but is not quite there yet. Look at the way he writes 'ont' for out. An 'n' is an upside down 'u'. Look at the attempt at 'whose': the group know that it begins with 'w', and make a very good try at the middle bit. Example 4 is really exciting. The children know that there is something odd about the middle of the word 'beginning', but they double the wrong letter. Look at the way they have spelt music, it's all there but in the wrong order. In 5, Sophie C is going to play the 'peyno', (and as she does it in the picture she says 'ready'). They have almost got a sound match for piano. An interesting and logical use of the letter 'y'. Example 8, spot on, just needing tidying with capital letters. What a lot these children know about language.

The teacher

Teachers have to learn to speak less, this is the message that you, as English coordinator, need to get across to your colleagues. They need to have the confidence to set up situations and to stand back and watch and listen to what happens. They must be aware of the educational benefits from such activities, the cooperation, turn taking, support, sharing of ideas, analysis, decision making and sharing of knowledge that such tasks produce.

 Every function in the child's development appears twice: first on the social level and later on the individual level; first between people (interpsychological) and then inside the child (intrapsychological). Vygotsky (1962)

We need to provide the opportunities for children to use speech to deepen their thought processes. To use 'talk' for learning. The English coordinator must make staff aware of this need and encourage them to take a united approach. This is possible with the youngest learners and if they start their schooling valuing 'talk' as a way to learn, then this consistency can spread up through the school with them.

Key Statement 3: The children need a language rich environment

The children

Lower school classrooms are filled with the written word. There are labels everywhere naming cupboards, paints, bricks, maths equipment, blocks, etc . . . how often are the children made aware of, and encouraged to read the signs? If we are not careful the displays in the room simply become decoration to the child. Written signs in the classroom should be a rich resource for learning about how print works. They should do more than name items, they should also inform. Print needs to be functional. Children need to be taken on regular 'print walks' around the classroom and the school. Take them along the corridor to read the teachers' names on the doors, the headteacher's office, the school office. Stop and read the notices that accompany children's work displayed on notice boards. Make them understand that being able to read helps you get around in life and explains things to you.

Books . . . our classrooms should be full of books to tempt children into reading. Classrooms are well stocked with scissors and glue, paintbrushes and paints but do we have enough books? We need books in classrooms not just in the school library. Children need to be able to browse, sample, select, share, enjoy. The one message that comes across from everyone involved in reading research is that children learn to read by reading lots and lots of texts: the more they read, the better they get. This is where the serial books that children get addicted to in later years are so useful and their value is often overlooked. By reading eight books in a series about a local football team the child gets a chance to practise and consolidate their reading at a certain level and in a form that interests them, before they move on. Most adults who are regular readers will share a background of the same sets of books in their primary school years, the Secret Seven, Famous Five, Hardy Boys, Nancy Drew. This is the staple diet that provides stamina for the gourmet feast. For the younger child this can be *Spot* books, the little bear books in Shigeo Watanabe's collection.

As English coordinator you need to have a clear policy about books in classrooms. This can either mean individual teachers selecting books from a centralised library area or perhaps boxes of books that circulate between a year band. Don't assume that all teachers are confident about selecting books for the classroom, they are not. You will need to be on hand to offer advice and help. It is a sad fact, but one that has to be faced, that not all teachers are 'bookish people'. Involve the children in the selection of the classroom books. Perhaps they could exchange ten or so books each week. Involve them in deciding which ones need renewing. In this way they become more aware of the wide range of available reading material.

Books need to be read regularly to the children so that when they select a book to take home to share it is a familiar book. In this way the 'reading' has a head start in the success stakes. Use recommendation notices, e.g. 'John really enjoyed reading *Mr Magnolia* by Quentin Blake because it was so funny.'

When the books are changed be sure to keep back those that some children still need to read regularly for consolidation. There is nothing wrong with a child reading a favourite book again and again. How many times have you been in a bookshop where a child is 'choosing' a book and the parent has not allowed them to buy the first choice because they have already read it at school. That is the very reason why the young child should be allowed to have it in order to build up a personal collection of books he or she can read. Spread the word to parents.

Use colourful alphabet friezes displayed not around the ceiling but somewhere where the children can touch the letters and trace the shape with their fingers, saying 'A, a, apple' as they do it. This helps them to become familiar with letter sounds and shapes.

The method

Let us just look at the example of notices that inform. One of the big problems in a well stocked infant classroom can be keeping everything tidy. Nagging the children to put things away in the right place is one way of doing it. Another is to include them in realising the reason why tidiness is important.

Get them to work in groups to talk about it for five minutes or so. Depending on the stage of the children in their writing development they could then write down their thoughts on big pieces of paper, one child being the scribe and the others helping with the mechanics of the writing, spelling etc. They can then pass on their work for other groups to read. After that they all return to the carpet, and, sitting round the easel, draw up a list of reasons why toys should be kept tidy. You can write the list for them, modelling writing, teaching skills in context. This can then be displayed prominently for all to read.

For example, one classroom had notices devised by the children with statements such as; 'Please clean your brush before you put it into a different colour because it's really annoying if you want red and get dirty brown.' The notices were read and changed regularly by children who were involved in the smooth running of classroom life. Again, the English coordinator notices such things by regularly visiting classrooms with wide open eyes.

The teachers

Teachers are not usually resistant to this sort of suggestion. Again, get a colleague to talk about using this kind of approach in the curriculum meeting. As English coordinator, you give the background information and let one of your peers deal with the interpretation. This goes back to tips on effective implementation of change that were dealt with in the previous section.

Getting teachers involved in effective group work in the classroom can take time, so don't be over-ambitious. Such sessions are often very noisy at first as the children adapt to a different way of being organised. Some teachers are frightened of losing control. If you have a really strong relationship of trust with the staff, offer to do a group work session with the teacher as an observer. Tell them to be aware of the strategies you are using and also to focus their attention on the involvement of the children. We seldom have the luxury of being a fly on the wall in our own classroom and it is an incredibly valuable opportunity to watch them all learning without being the one organising everything and dealing with queries etc. The children will wonder what is going on, so tell them that another teacher is going to teach them and you are going to watch the way they learn. Tell them not to come and speak to you as you need to concentrate hard. Involve the children in what is happening.

If teachers can see the advantages for their own children then they are often more willing to try because it is not a direct request to alter their teaching style, but a focus on a more effective learning experience for the children. To be able to do this sort of thing means negotiation to free you from your own class for an hour or so.

Key Statement 4: All reading and writing experiences should be child centred, purposeful and meaningful

The children

The ways that young children make sense of print are intriguing. Everyone involved in reading research has been caught by a fascination for this process. Everyone is doing it for the good of children, but the teaching of reading has always been an area of contention. What you need to do is to read as widely as you can from all perspectives and then follow leads that fit the needs of your children. The tightly structured 'Literacy Hour' provides a starting point for schools that have not yet set their own priorities for what must happen each day. This will lead towards a shared understanding of what we know about the reading process and a negotiated, agreed level of consistency of approach so that children are not confused when they move from class to class and method to method.

The great 'phonic' debate has dominated discussion for decades. Do children need phonics knowledge to learn to read? The work of Goswami and Bryant (1990) would suggest that it is not phonic knowledge but phonemic awareness that differentiates the early reader from the struggler. It is the ability to hear the separate phonemes in words that is important. Children can be drilled, rather like performing animals, to respond to flash cards of initial sounds, but that doesn't mean that the child can separate the 'a'-ness of 'a' when it is located in a word. Margaret Donaldson (1978) suggests that such rapid 'schooling' of phonic recognition deprives the child of time to consider possibilities of interpretation, if he does not know immediately then he will guess wildly and he won't be aware of the development of his thought processes. Words on a page occur in context and this is what the child needs.

It would seem that a knowledge of phonics is of far more use to the young child as an aid to early writing. Uta Frith (1980) maintains that the relationship between phonemes and graphemes is acquired first for spelling and then for reading, thus the child begins to read by eye, logographically, and to spell by ear alphabetically. Bryant and Bradley (1980) tell us of children who could read 'light' but not write it, and write 'bun' but not read it. Refer to Goswami and Bryant's work on onset and rime. They found that children could cope with the initial sound, the onset, and the end grouping of letters, the rime, but that anything in the middle caused great problems for most beginning readers.

It is possible to synthesise all this research and come up with a seemingly obvious concept that children are taught the letter sounds to help them initially to become writers and they become readers relying on sight. As this knowledge becomes embedded in the child, the phonic strength acquired for writing will later aid the child in word attack skills and the strong visual awareness developed in early reading will help when phonic knowledge is not enough to cope with the peculiarities of the English spelling system.

Something to beware of when you are reading research about the subject. Children start formal schooling at different ages and therefore at different stages of development from country to country. In North America and many European countries, children tend to begin formal schooling at least a year later than British children. These children with more pre-school, informal literacy learning have probably all attained a degree of phonemic awareness and are ready to absorb phonic instruction. We tend to write about 'the beginner' without realising the difference in age and development of these internationally researched 'beginners'.

Colin Harrison (1992) suggests that to become a reader a child needs to acquire four different kinds of knowledge. Knowledge of how the world works, in order to understand the situation of the story being read. Knowledge of how language works, with the forms that authors use and the syntactic structures common to storytelling. Knowledge of how stories work. For example, Carol Fox (1993) in her book *At the Very Edge of the Forest, The Influence of Storytelling on Children*, shares accounts of how the stories children are told in their pre-school days show up in their later storytellings, writing and ability to predict outcomes when reading. Lastly knowledge of how books work. This can go from the simple knowledge of which way up to hold the book and whether to start from the front or the back, to what the Literacy Framework calls 'sentence level' where knowledge about print, capital letters, question marks, speech marks, are specifically taught from the earliest stages.

The texts we use with children can hold the key to enjoyment in reading. There is such a wealth of wonderful material nowadays that it is often difficult to keep up with all the best new publications.

When buying texts to help children become readers the list of criteria for selection that Liz Waterland (1989) developed is a sound guide. As English coordinator these could certainly help in the selection process.

1 Can the story however simple be read aloud by an adult in a natural, interested way?
2 Is the language natural, sensible, predictable and meaningful?
3 Is there some special attribute, humour, pattern, high quality of illustration and colour that will appeal to children?
4 Do the text and illustrations work together dynamically?
5 Has the book been written by an author who wanted to write a book for children?

It is no coincidence that the favourite books of young readers are those produced by author illustrators like John Burningham, Pat Hutchins, Ruth Brown, Anthony Browne, Maurice Sendak, Babette Cole, Tony Ross, David McKee, Rod Campbell, Eric Carle, the Ahlbergs, the list could go on and on. What schools need are multiple copies of these texts that work. Teachers who use texts like these predominantly in their classrooms need to be very knowledgeable about directing the child to the right book at the right time. Yes, children need to have freedom of choice, but reading a good story to the class and then saying 'Who would like to take this home in their book bag?' will guarantee that the child who you want to read it will undoubtedly put their hand up and you can choose them to take it.

It's a good idea to let children select two or three books to take home to read. Then have a selection of bookmarks with 'Please Read This With Me', or 'Please Read This To Me', or 'I Can Read This Myself', written on the top. These markers can be negotiated with the child when the books are selected. They also act as an early warning sign if things are becoming stressful because the child who insists on only selecting books to be read to her is probably experiencing problems. Children need access to books at different levels. After a busy day at school young learners do not need to be 'stretched' at home like pieces of elastic. Sometimes they need books to browse through, sometimes familiar comfortable favourites to share and sometimes, when confidence is high, a new book where they can apply their knowledge and skills. Bookmarks like these can also be beneficial to parents who do not always know what to do with the books when they come home.

Another good idea, as English coordinator, is to encourage the teachers to allow the children to write a comment in the dialogue book that goes home with the books. This includes the children in their own learning and makes them feel part of the whole process.

It all leads to an acceptance that the strands of literacy should not be separated. Reading and writing, like speaking and listening, are inseparable processes. We learn to read by writing and to write by reading and to read by reading and to write by writing and round and round it goes in a spiral of learning with the child building on and constructing knowledge.

Writing, from the very first pencil mark on the paper, gives children a means of expressing meaning. They should be encouraged to express their own ideas with confidence and to know that their efforts will be received by a supportive mentor who will give the child the confidence to further experiment with this new medium of expression. They have to be allowed to try for themselves. As English coordinator you need to be sure that all teachers at Key Stage 1 understand this role. One way to do this is to separate the teaching of letter formation as a distinct area of skill teaching. The work of Cripps and Cox (1989) on the links between good spellers and fluent handwriters should be considered. They maintain that through the practice of writing letter patterns in joined writing, those patterns become fixed and are repeated automatically. Encourage teachers to spend time in regular, concentrated modelling demonstrations to develop spelling awareness, focus attention on patterns, laugh with them at the silliness of some English spelling and then leave the children alone to try to write by themselves and with each other. The teachers must then respond with gentleness and guide the child with sensitivity to write more and be aware of the conventions of writing. Encourage teachers to talk to the children individually about their writing in order to sustain progress.

Brian Cambourne (1988) summarised the needs of the learner as follows.

Learners need:
1 immersion in appropriate texts;
2 appropriate demonstrations;
3 the responsibility for making decisions about when, how and what they read and write;
4 high expectations about themselves as readers and writers;
5 freedom to approximate forms of reading and writing;
6 time to engage in the acts of reading and writing;

7 opportunities to employ developing reading and writing skills and knowledge in meaningful contexts;

8 responses and feedback from knowledgeable others which both support and inform their attempts at constructing meaning using written language.

Spelling

Some mention here needs to be made about spelling because it is an issue that is bound to crop up and it is as well to have a sound knowledge about spelling acquisition. Many teachers have said that the most useful guide to an understanding of the spelling process is that given by Richard Gentry (1987). In his book *Spel is a Four Letter Word*, he tells how as a child he became school, town, state and inter-state spelling champion yet on entry to university he appalled his tutor by his inability to spell. He became a 'spelling champion' with the assistance of his grandmother, who helped him to learn lists of words which he would reproduce in a test situation, but could not use correctly a week or two later. In later life he became fascinated by the spelling process and identified five distinct spelling stages. As English coordinator introduce these to your colleagues and perhaps suggest that you monitor the children in line with the Gentry stages.

Precommunicative At first the child produces 'scribble' writing as a result of watching adults or peers writing. These early attempts often show a knowledge of left to right orientation and spacing between words. The writing flows as in a cursive style and is not represented in separate letters as in printing. (A point that Cripps and Cox highlight in their work about the links between cursive writing and spelling.)

At this stage the children display no knowledge of letter sound relationships and if letters, numbers or even musical notation are written they are used randomly. The child does not differentiate between upper and lower case letters, in fact upper case seems to dominate.

Semiphonetic Gentry considers this to be the time when the child begins to grasp the idea that letters have sounds which represent the sounds in words. At this stage the child can produce a partial phonetic representation of the word being spelled with only a few letters being used, usually the consonants because these are easier to hear than vowels. This is the time when the child makes use of the letter name to represent the sound. e.g. U (you) R (are). Knowledge is being gained about the alphabet and the letter forms and the child is beginning to use spaces between the words. This is the stage when the teacher should be providing opportunities for playing language games, learning rhymes and poems and giving children every chance to concentrate on the sounds of the language.

Phonetic At this stage the child is able to provide a complete mapping of the letter sound relationships in the word being spelled. Here the work of Read (1987) on 'creative spellers' should be visited, for he suggests that children use techniques that adults have long since forgotten. Problems occur with nasals before consonants e.g. think of the number of times children omit the 'n' in 'went'. It is not due to carelessness. It is because the 'n' is a swallowed sound and is hard to hear. Letters are assigned strictly on the basis of sound. The child generally makes use of word spacing, but there are still times when a child might be struggling with 'once upon a time' thinking that it was all one word. At this stage the child shows a mixture of stages with some words spelled phonetically, some semiphonetically and some correctly.

Transitional This is when the child undergoes a transition from a reliance on sound to represent words to a much greater reliance on visual representation. It is also the time when the child's reading is making rapid progress. His knowledge of the letter sound relationship will assist his reading and his visually acquired reading skills will further his awareness of the way words are spelled. At this stage the child makes use of vowels in every syllable and uses vowel combinations such as 'ai', 'ea', 'ee'. The use of letter names rather than sounds dies out and the child can combine vowel and consonant for example 'el' in elephant instead of 'L'. Whether he can cope with the 'ph' representation of the 'f' sound is another matter. If he can, then he can probably spell 'phish'! The child has now come to terms with nasals and can put the 'n' in went. The child is able to use the silent 'e' as in 'bite' rather than 'bit'. Use is made of learned inflectional endings like 'ing', 'est', 'ed', and 'ies'. This is the time when the child can enjoy the nonsense of the 'ight' words and use them with confidence. Ordering can sometimes be a problem. The child has 'house' in his visual memory but it is written as 'huose'. Alternative spellings for the same sound appear as in 'eightee', 'lasee', 'rane', and 'sail'/'sale'.

Correct Not many Key Stage 1 children will reach this level, but it is worth completing the overview. At this stage the child has collected a large body of known words including the correct spelling of prefixes, suffixes, contractions, and compound words. There is accuracy in the use of silent consonants for example in 'climb' and 'knee', and in the use of double consonants like 'hopping', 'beginning', 'running'. The child has come to terms with homophones and knows that they have different spellings according to their meanings. Also at this stage the child is aware when a word doesn't look right, thus control is gained over irregular words. Control of spelling resources such as the dictionary, thesaurus and spell check on the computer will have been mastered.

Traditionally spelling instruction has been viewed as a separate formal lesson involving the learning of lists of words. It is now believed that spelling generalisations are enhanced when spelling is regarded as a skill of writing.

The image we have of ourselves as spellers stays with us often throughout our lives. If a child is told repeatedly that he is a 'poor speller', then that is what he will remain throughout his life. A positive self image is very important. As English coordinator do encourage the teachers to take a positive, knowledgeable attitude when dealing with spelling errors.

The method

So what can you do as English coordinator to encourage teachers to put this knowledge into practice? Well, they can do a lot to help children to develop phonemic awareness. Children who come into school being able to recite nursery rhymes were found to make faster reading progress. Teach lots of rhymes, jingles and poems. Use Big Books which highlight phonemic awareness. For example *Rat-a-Tat-Tat*, by Jill Eggleton, is an excellent example of a text that can be used to assess the phonemic awareness of young learners. It also has all the elements of a good text for beginners in that it incorporates rhythm, rhyme, repetition, prediction and eye catching, informative illustrations by Rodney McRae.

On a subsequent reading of this text with the children, every now and then change the wording from 'Rat-a-tat-tat' to 'Rat-a-fat-cat who is that?' Or 'Bat-a-fat-rat who is that?' Watch the children's faces. See who laughs instantly, who thinks a bit and then laughs, who hasn't got a clue what the others are laughing at and laughs half heartedly so as not to be left out. These are the children who cannot yet differentiate between similar consonant sounds. They are the ones who need to be monitored carefully for their level of phonemic awareness is lagging behind that of the majority of the class. Use clever texts like this for on-going formative assessment that is a natural part of the daily literacy routine, not an additional burden.

As a follow up to the reading and direct teaching of the text, encourage teachers to allow the children to make their own books using the same pattern. Tell them to write the pattern on large sheets of paper and display them all around the room so that the children have to look, remember, write and check. (Margaret Peters's visual spelling routine, with the addition of 'remember'.)

Here we have children engaged in thinking, creating, reading and writing for the purpose of making their own little books. They are given a structure, but freedom within that structure to be creative. This is a writing activity that follows quite specific focused teaching. The child can stop at one example, others may continue and produce three or four. Children enjoy activities like this and learn a lot from them. Coordinators can then show teachers the potential for structured play activities. The children can make their books come alive in the home corner where they will speak and listen and use the taught language items, thus reinforcing their learning.

Another example is of Rachel, aged 5 and a half who wrote a very personal story as a result of the shared reading of the Big Book version of *I Went Walking*, by Sue Williams. At first the book was read for sheer enjoyment and pleasure. It was then read a second time looking specifically at punctuation, spelling and verb tenses. There was very concentrated, focused teaching and learning taking place. On the third reading the children split into two groups and one group asked the question and the others replied by reading and following the text. It was then suggested that they should all make a small book about 'I went walking' and describe the things they saw. The children had experienced the language structure being taught, were given the chance to process that information and were now being asked to apply it in a contextualised form.

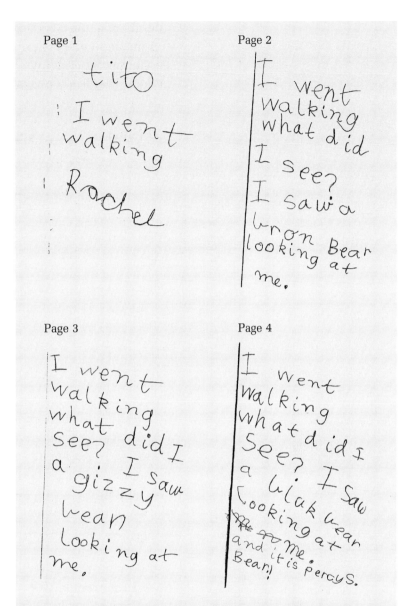

Page 1

tito
I went
walking
Rachel

Page 2

I went
walking
what did
I see?
I saw a
bron Bear
looking at
me.

Page 3

I went
walking
what did I
see? I saw
a gizzy
bean
looking at
me.

Page 4

I went
walking
what did I
see? I saw
a lilak bean
looking at
me. and it is percy S.
Bean!

Rachel changed it to a personal dialogue and wrote,

I went walking
what did I see?

Note her attempt to spell 'title', her ability to write her name in cursive writing, the use of punctuation, the question mark and the full stop. Here is a child acquiring knowledge about language and displaying the ability to use that knowledge at a very early age. It is also interesting that she has restricted her text to meeting bears, and rounds it up with an encounter with the classroom teddy bear, Percy S. Bear.

Coordinators need to encourage teachers to capitalise on the full potential of a text so that they exploit every teaching angle possible without killing the children's interest. This can perhaps best be seen when put into a chart.

story	no. of children	nature of text	grammatical features	word awareness	application	extension
Big Book version of *I Went Walking* by Sue Williams	whole class sitting around easel	repetitive pattern, statement, question, response	capital letters, question marks, full stops, past tense . . . I saw, what did you see?	repeated pattern, colours, animals	writing own version within framework of repetitive text	sharing books with each other, classroom display, display around school

Often the best early reading material a child can have is a book that they have written themselves and if that book follows a pattern that maximises learning, so much the better.

The teachers

There is so much that teachers need to know. Where do you, the English coordinator, begin? One way is to set aside part of your budget to develop the English section of the staff library. Go for some good texts on the theoretical side and as many 'teacher friendly', practical, useful books as you can find. Teachers have so many demands on their time that keeping abreast of recent research is often one area that gets put on semi-permanent hold. Try to persuade a different staff member to read and review new acquisitions. Read them all yourself and promote the really useful chapters. Photocopy the cover, there surely would be no objection to that, and surround it with speech bubbles highlighting relevant sections. Negotiate perhaps ten minutes at the beginning of staff meetings to promote new texts.

Save articles from the educational press and circulate them to colleagues or start a folder for reference. Take out a subscription for the school with journals relating to English matters.

Teachers also need to read and be familiar with the full range of children's books that are available in the school. Start displaying new editions in the staffroom for people to browse through at break times.

Develop a computer file of texts that work well for readers at different developmental stages. This is a really useful thing to do. For example, have a list of books that include lots of natural repetition, like *I Went Walking* by Sue Williams, *Brown Bear, Brown Bear, What do You See?* by Bill Martin, *The Dark, Dark Wood* by Ruth Brown, *We're Going on a Bear Hunt* by Michael Rosen.

So many things to do, but it can't all be achieved at once. Take small steps to begin with and have an overview of how you want the staff to develop. What you want is a staff who see the development of literacy skills as being the very core of all their teaching. They need to find ways to exploit every teaching situation to achieve this.

Chapter 5

How does all this fit within the Literacy Framework?

Reinforcing practice

Many schools and teachers are concerned that all the energy they have put into developing their early English curriculum and practice will now be lost in the quest for the national Literacy Strategy. This is not the case. The Literacy Framework supports all of the examples in response to the key statements above. The planning documentation within the Literacy Framework shows the importance of the range expected for children and reinforces the practice discussed here by emphasising that teachers should strive to promote such opportunities for children. What the Framework does is to ensure that experiences are put into order, that nothing is left out and, that by setting aside time, teachers really do focus upon some aspects that, in the past had been fitted in if possible.

For example, the Framework emphasises the importance of grammatical awareness from the reception year and, as they enter Key Stage 1, children should be 'taught to draw on their grammatical awareness'. In Year 2, children should be 'taught to recognise and take account of commas and exclamation marks when reading aloud and to re-read their own writing for punctuation'. Where such issues have been talked about and recommended, they are now required and when they are required is defined. This means that parallel classes will get the same teaching and the same expectations. For so long schools have talked about children re-reading their own work when, for some teachers, the reality is that they re-work every child's efforts whilst battling with the ever-growing queue.

What is developing in the Framework is a series of recommendations about the best way to teach certain aspects, say, of grammar. The task of the coordinator will be to help teachers to decide which approach is most relevant and useful to them in their situation.

The other task of the coordinator is to draw up a plan of how other aspects of English work can run alongside the Literacy Hour. The Literacy Hour is the 'on-going' unit of work. The 'blocked' and the 'linked' units need to be determined to help the whole picture gel together. So, for instance, how does children's imaginative play fit into the scheme of things? How can aspects of play be fitted in so that they feed and feed off the hour per day?

In one school a Year 2 teacher made Maurice Sendak's classic *Where The Wild Things Are* the centre of her teaching over a number of weeks. She fully exploited the text and the children's interest so that the literacy teaching spilled over into all the learning. Her planning looked like this.

Where The Wild Things Are by Maurice Sendak

English	Art	Maths	Geography	Drama/play	Hidden curriculum
Enjoyment and involvement with the text. Read and re-read committing some sections to heart, guided writing, 'If I met a Wild Thing . . . ?'	Create the land of the wild things within the classroom, i.e. vines hanging from the ceiling, trees all around, Max's 'royal' tent as the 'home corner', a boat preferably in the book corner so that the children can be Max, but also have somewhere special to read.	In and out of weeks and almost over a year . . . work on time.	Oceans and other lands. The idea of travelling through time, it's breakfast time in UK but teatime in Australia etc.	Endless possibilities for drama; as an assembly or bigger production; Links with music, creating original music as an accompaniment. Free play in the boat and Max's tent.	How to deal with anger, punishment, forgiveness.

Topics and themes in school often roll along and then 'fizzle' out because there is no event to mark their closing. In this case the children had a 'Wild Things' picnic as the culmination. They made themselves colourful 'Wild Things' T-shirts and had a wild rumpus to celebrate the end of a successful period of intense learning.

In Year 1, term 1, children are to work on 'signs, labels, captions, lists, and instructions'. Where better to support the hour than in the shop, the cafe, the garage or the vet's? If we expand the suggestion of the vet's then we can remove the home corner equipment and turn the area into a vet's surgery.

Starting point	Resources	Speaking and listening	Reading	Writing
A story, *Six Dinner Sid* by Inga Moore.	2 tables, chairs for waiting room, telephone, white coats etc.	Children have to phone to make appointment, describe what is wrong with pet, use specific language.	Signs around the surgery e.g. about controlling pets, having to wait etc., appointment cards, leaflets about caring for pets.	Secretary keeping appointment book, vet writing diagnosis, get well cards for pet!

There are endless possibilities but the coordinator will need to encourage colleagues to think laterally and imaginatively.

The essence of the strategy is displayed diagrammatically. All of this is covered in 'what you need to know'. As the Literacy Framework (p. 4) says, we do not need over-cautious teachers. A task for the coordinator is to exploit the opportunity created by the development and use it well.

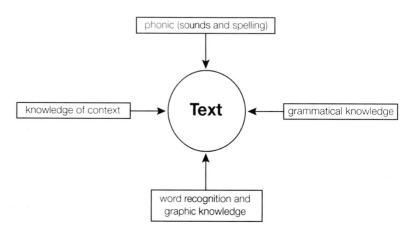

Links with other subjects

In the early days of National Curriculum implementation, teachers of early years children were alarmed that they were being asked to include so much in the curriculum that basic skills would suffer. This showed a belief in the segmentation of the curriculum. In busy, bustling infant classrooms there aren't clearly defined breaks between 'language activities' and history or geography . . . are there? Surely what we are actually doing is developing literacy skills through the medium of history or geography. Yes, children are acquiring a knowledge dimension in other areas, but they are doing it by speaking and listening, reading and writing.

Let's look at this through the example of a piece of investigative work in a history 'lesson' with a primary 2 class at the beginning of the academic year.

The session was designed to pay attention to AT1 in history, sequencing objects and events. This is how the teacher documented the experience.

Becoming a Toy Detective

(The child has written: Toy detectives hunt for clues. Has it come straight from the toy shop? What clues can you find? My clues are holes in his ears. He's been squished his neck has gone floppy.)

Desired outcomes: To develop an awareness of the need to look closely for evidence. To question and to seek solutions based on the evidence discovered. To develop historical enquiry.

Lesson planning: To examine artefacts in an attempt to classify them in order of age.

Starting point: The known. The children were all asked to bring a soft toy to school that they had owned since they were born. They would also be working with four toys of unknown age and would be asked to compare and contrast them and then attempt to put them in order of age.

Organisation: The children worked in groups of four and first of all introduced their own toy to the group.

They were given five minutes talking time and were then stopped and told to look closely for clues that would show that their toy had not just arrived from the toy shop. The children then came together as a class to share their observations. The four unknown teddies were introduced.

1 A brand new teddy bought the day before with a price tag and hook.
2 A 12 year old ET belonging to my daughter.
3 An 18 year old Blue Ted belonging to my son.
4 A 46 year old rabbit which is mine.

The children then stayed in their groups and started to draw and write about their own teddy whilst one group at a time investigated the four ancient examples.
They loved the idea of being toy detectives hunting for clues. Clearly displayed was the question, 'Has it come straight from the toy shop?' as well as a list of useful words based on the children's observations of their own toy, old, arms, fluffy, new, legs, fur, floppy, stuffing, hair, neck, stitches, mouth, whiskers, torn, tail.

Time: About 1 hour.

Resources used: Just the teddies and magnifying glasses.

Results: This was the list of evidence that the children found. They sat around the easel to share their discoveries and 'helped me' to write up the results.

Christmas Bear
1 He has a hook where he was hanging in the shop.
2 He has a price tag.
3 His fur is clean and soft and fluffy.

4   He has a new bow.
5   His button works!
Verdict: New

ET
1   His eyes are missing.
2   His arms and legs are floppy because he has been loved so much.
3   His fur is dirty and it isn't fluffy any more.
Verdict: Old.

Blue Ted
1   He's ever so dirty.
2   He's lost a lot of fur.
3   His stuffing has gone hard.
4   He looks like he's been loved for longer than ET.
Verdict: Older

Wilfy Rabbit
1   His stuffing is coming out.
2   He's got lots of patches.
3   The ears are chewed and falling off.
4   He's got holes everywhere.
Verdict: Oldest

This involved lots of talking and shared writing with the teacher as scribe.

Evaluation of the lesson: It was a magical experience with total involvement, focusing on the issues, thinking clearly, looking for evidence, expressing opinions, backing these up with close observations.

Quality teaching/learning? The children were totally involved and oblivious to anything going on outside their immediate group.

They were working collaboratively and functioning efficiently as a group.
The deputy headteacher looked in to see what they were doing and they were able to tell her clearly exactly what they were doing and why they were doing it.
Parent feedback was requested and six replied enthusiastically saying their children had gone home and given a detailed account. One mentioned that all the family teddies had to be lined up and investigated. Another said that, 'Our teddy was alive before us because it must have been made just before we were born.'

What had they learned about history? They had been working at AT1 sequencing objects.

They realised that history is all about looking for evidence and making assumptions based on that evidence.

What a lot those children learned, and what a lot of good English teaching was going on amidst the history. Look at the way this young child attempted to spell 'hole'. He was bringing his knowledge of spelling 'wh' words to work out how to spell 'hole' or maybe he had found the word 'whole' somewhere. The children in this class were used to being word detectives as well as history detectives. In fairness this is easier to do at Key Stage 1 than 2, but think about this, history provides the teacher with exactly the right context to teach about verbs in the past tense. This will be particularly important the more children you have with English as an additional language.

Children with English as an additional language

A lot of negative things are said about the problems such children pose. Look at the other side of the issue. Here you have children who have already acquired one language and are well on their way to mastering another. Young children have an incredible ability to acquire language; this natural ability diminishes the older we get. What they need is immersion in the new language and this is where problems can occur. If the proportion of non-mother tongue speakers dominates, then there is a challenge for the school. It's not the children that are the challenge but the method of dealing with the situation. As English coordinator you have to face this situation head on and point out to teachers that you can't necessarily go through a career teaching in the same way, your teaching has to reflect the needs of the children you teach. The problem is not with the children but often with the resistance of the teachers to changing their approach.

A knowledge of the structure of the predominant mother tongue language is essential — not an ability to speak it necessarily, but an awareness of how the spoken and written language works. Is it a language that has tenses, syllables? Is the written form logographic or alphabetic? What is the orientation of the printed word? left to right? right to left? vertical? horizontal?

It is often said by the ill informed that such children come into school with 'no language' . . . No, they come into school with a rich knowledge of language, it's just a different language.

Sometimes a story helps. 'Story' has been used by educators for centuries to get points across. Narrative is a very powerful medium of thought. Barbara Hardy (1977) in her essay 'Narrative as a primary act of mind' maintains that storytelling plays a crucial role in the development of the thought processes and has a major role in our sleeping and waking lives.

> *For we dream in narrative, daydream in narrative, remember, anticipate, hope, despair, doubt, plan, revise, criticise, construct, gossip, learn, hate, and love by narrative. In order really to live, we make up stories about ourselves and others, about the personal as well as the social past and future.*

So having provided the theoretical reason we can proceed to look at the teaching method.

Once there was a school, an inner city Catholic school with a history going back 70 years or more. Over the years the people living in the catchment area of this school changed. It became a place where Muslim immigrants from Pakistan settled, set up home and raised their children. These children went to school and very soon they numbered 95 per cent of the school population. Many of the teachers continued teaching in the way they had always taught, and the very youngest children became quieter and quieter. Some said they had no language so how can we teach them to read and write. The prayers written in large letters around the room held little meaning for these children even if they could read them. They needed a learning environment geared towards their needs and they were not really getting it. Where were the books, big, colourful books to make the children smile and give them the desire to find the meaning of the strange printed words? No, these children 'were not ready for books, they hadn't got any language, what good would books be?'

One day, along came an outsider with faith in children and awe at the ability of the very young to learn new things, far more quickly than wiser adults. With her she brought a large brightly coloured papier mâché elephant. An elephant dressed in the garish trappings of a festival. A sad elephant, who had just arrived in the UK and could speak no English. He needed some kind children to help him learn English quickly. The children smiled and with great gentleness welcomed him and instantly loved him. In her bag this visitor had a collection of books about elephants, every book she could find in the library and the biggest and most beautifully illustrated of those books had a text written in a language the visitor could not speak. So she sat the children down, with the elephant, and she told them the story of the pictures. Half way through the story one small, 5 year old boy put up his hand and in a distinctly irritated voice said, 'Miss, Miss, you are telling us the wrong story, you are not telling us the story of the words'. 'Do you know the story of the words?' she asked. 'Yes,' he said. 'Would you like to read it to us?' And very seriously the small boy read the story to his classmates and the elephant. At the end of the story the visitor said, 'Where did you learn to read?' 'At the mosque Miss, on Saturdays.' 'How many of you can read this story?' Most of the hands went up.

The visitor smiled. Here were a group of children who already knew about the reading process, who had already made that leap from the spoken word to the printed word. With careful guidance and help they

---

could make that leap in language number two. So they started by making a book, a big book together, a book about their own elephant who had come to live in their classroom. And the children drew pictures, big colourful pictures and the visitor wrote the words, the words that these children with no language told her to write. And then they all read the book.

What was it that produced the spark which made these hesitant children relax and use English? It was something 'un-school' like, familiar yet different, infinitely appealing with a parallel to their own lives. It required imagination and creativity on the part of the 'visitor' who had not forgotten how it felt to be lost and confused. It also needed the intuition to see things through the eyes of a child. It required the 'use of English' to have a purpose. It required more than the acquisition of new vocabulary; it required the application of knowledge within a motivating context.

Children with special needs

As Key Stage 1 coordinator you are going to have to make decisions about children within this category. Identifying them is the first task. Certainly by the end of their first year in school children will give clues as to their level of ability. There are things to watch out for.

With potential strugglers:
- is there a mismatch between apparent verbal intelligence and performance in reading and writing activities?
- is the child developing phonemic awareness?
- can she remember the words of songs and simple rhymes?
- can she remember a message and deliver it correctly?
- is there evidence of letter reversals and mirror writing?
- is she building up a sight knowledge of familiar words?
- can she match sounds to letters?
- does she show interest in reading or is the self esteem sinking?
- can she concentrate through group modelling of reading and writing sessions?

With the potentially gifted:
- does the child seem unmotivated by things that appeal to the others?
- does she seem to be in a dream for much of the day?
- does she spend a lot of time reading alone and playing alone?

- does she get frustrated that others don't understand what she takes as understood?
- can she think in the abstract without need of apparatus?

As coordinator you need to have a system for noting such evidence that children display, whilst at the same time accepting that it is difficult at this early age to know whether there is a learning problem in the case of the strugglers, or just a developmental delay. Children get started with literacy at different times, but certainly by the end of Key Stage 1 children with problems should be easier to locate and a plan of action can be put in place. If the teacher is concerned, then the parents who know the child far better, will probably be sharing the same concerns. Encourage the teacher to talk to them without creating alarm and panic and gently suggest things that they can be doing at home to help. Parents should see the need to create quality time to sit down and share a known book, looking at the pictures pointing to the text, concentrating on the known, and building trust and confidence.

How do the teachers feel about the subject?

The teaching of literacy skills is such a fundamental element of being an early years teacher that we assume that all teachers are enthusiastic and confident in the area, but are they? To be a good reading teacher do you need to enjoy reading yourself? Good reading teachers are often those who are keen to share their love of books and their enthusiasm rubs off on the children. Do the teachers enjoy writing? Are they good models for the children? How about attitudes to spelling? If there is a lack of knowledge of the process then teachers tend to flounder and have no consistent approach. Does the teacher experience problems with spelling and have a low spelling self esteem? This actually might sound strange, but often adults who struggled to acquire literacy skills as a child can become far more intuitive, sensitive teachers as adults because they will remember more about the learning process themselves. As English coordinator you need to encourage your headteacher to place some of your most skilled teachers in these early years classrooms for this is where the pattern of the child's learning is established.

Everything described in this Part is a foundation upon which the Literacy Framework is built. Children need regular consistent teaching of the skills that will make them literate. It is hoped that English coordinators will understand these foundational beliefs in order to lead their colleagues in this national approach. Its success needs enthusiasm and confident input.

Part three

Developing and maintaining a policy for English at KS 1

Chapter 6
Producing a policy document

Chapter 7
Planning

Producing a policy document

Why do we need a policy document for English?

A policy document gives you the chance to express your school's beliefs, practices and visions for the future within the context of the school's statutory obligations. It is a document unique to the needs of your school. A good policy document will establish continuity and consistency and will be developed by a team of colleagues intent on reflecting the nature of practice within the school. There are many valid reasons for quality time being spent in establishing such a document. A good policy document will evolve over a period of time as priority areas are focused upon, reviewed, discussed, agreed and written up.

A curriculum policy document:
■ will focus staff attention on professional issues as a result of having to sit down and think about what they believe in;
■ will have everything written down ensuring that verbal agreements are not misinterpreted;
■ will be there for new staff and supply teachers as an introduction to the English teaching in the school;
■ will provide OFSTED, LEAs, governors and parents with evidence of your school's intentions in the curriculum area;
■ will maintain beliefs in the event of a change of headteacher or English coordinator until such time as they feel changes are in order;

■ will be reviewed and updated as new innovations become standard practice.

In writing the document staff will:
■ get a clearer picture of the teaching and learning strategies favoured by your school;
■ be fully aware of the part they have to play in the maintenance of consistency throughout the school;
■ have the opportunity to debate issues before they become school policy;
■ have involvement and therefore ownership which will lead to a greater sense of responsibility for the implementation of such a document.

Where to begin?

As in all aspects of change this is totally dependent on where you, the coordinator and your school are now. It will also depend on:
■ how long you have been in the post;
■ whether or not you are new to the school;
■ whether there is an existing policy document in place.

The first thing the coordinator will need to do is connected with the audit mentioned in Part 1. You need to spend time getting to know exactly what is going on in the area of English teaching in the school. This will entail close observation when visiting classrooms, talking to teachers and talking to children. If there is a policy document in existence:
■ does it match with the practice that you are able to observe;
■ do the teachers seem to have a shared understanding and a common vision of the needs of the children;
■ does the statement match the teaching approaches?

Perhaps the existing document will only need fine tuning, in which case you are lucky. However, it may need a major review. The most effective way to approach this issue will be to assume that you are starting from scratch and therefore focus attention on the elements of a curriculum policy for English.

What to include?

I Philosophy

You need to begin with a clear statement of the school's philosophy about the learning and teaching process and the desired learning environment the school is striving to achieve. This will be common to all subject areas and is something that can be addressed by the whole staff. This will obviously have to be instigated by the headteacher as it is a statement crucial to the development of the school. There is no need to call a special meeting, mention it in a staff meeting and then circulate everyone with the questionnaire. Request replies within a certain number of days and then the coordinators can sit down and form a common statement in light of the suggestions of colleagues. This again can be circulated for comment. It should then come up for endorsement at a staff meeting. You will then have to establish a clear list of beliefs about English teaching. This will include a statement about:

- what you value in a literate child;
- how the community values literacy;
- how the school aims to reflect the cultural richness of the children;
- how the worth of each girl and boy is to be monitored.

2 Background

Many schools include a section on the background of the school and the approaches that have been used over the years. Such information is very useful to new members of staff who are more easily able then to assimilate the practice with the situation. For example, one coordinator felt it necessary to explain the different approaches to the teaching of reading that had been applied in the school over the previous ten years or so. She wrote:

 In September 1986 the school began to alter the way in which reading was taught. A gradual change was anticipated but this did not take into account the enthusiasm of the children and things moved a lot faster than was envisaged. During the

previous year the school was fortunate to have the chance for whole staff in-service, run by an enlightened primary adviser. It was an excellent course which made staff think deeply about their practice in light of recent research. After the course, teachers read further, deepened their knowledge and as a team, came to the conclusion that change was needed. The parents were kept fully informed as to what changes were taking place and why they were deemed necessary. So the school moved into an era when large stocks of multiple copies of picture books, that help children become motivated, enthusiastic readers, became the backbone of reading experience.

It is beneficial to see the path to literacy that the school has taken because the expectations of the community will undoubtedly be based on what has gone before. It is also quite possible that in a surprisingly short space of time, children of previous pupils will be attending the school. You can then reassure, with confidence, the parent who felt that what was good for her is good enough for her child.

3 Objectives

Here you can include the statutory objectives laid down by the National Curriculum and the Literacy Framework together with any others that you as a staff feel are important.

4 Guidelines

This is the real nitty gritty where the coordinator spells out what is to happen in each classroom in the school, thus maintaining consistency. They will not be imposed guidelines to those staff members present at their inception, but they will be to new teachers joining the school so bear that in mind when inducting new staff. These guidelines will have to be built up and added to as each priority area is addressed. In this way the policy is seen as an evolving process that builds on established strength. Here are suggestions for the topics to include in your guidelines.

Activity 6: Suggested topics to include in policy guidelines

Highlighting daily happenings

This is where the Literacy Hour comes in. The Framework provides for a daily happening throughout the primary phase. The structure of the daily, hourly happening is prescribed and the content is offered to be put into each session. The scheme, therefore, is prescribed. For some teachers this is a big concern. Images of being dictated to, reduced professionalism and having no discretion proliferate.

Some would question whether we need a scheme when the Literacy Framework is provided for us. However the key issue is whether the Framework is the whole of the English curriculum. Certainly in terms of a school's Literacy Hours there does not seem much point in revamping what has been produced in the literacy scheme of work. However consideration by the coordinator must be given to what aspects of the English curriculum will not be covered in the Literacy Hours. Certainly Speaking and Listening are not detailed despite a couple of sentences arguing for the important ways in which they impact on literacy development. There is also no mention of drama. Two aspects of English for which 'additional time may also be needed' (p. 14) are
- continuing the practice of reading to the class;
- pupils' own independent reading for interest and pleasure.

What is lacking in the framework is, though, the notion of how these other aspects of English will relate to the Literacy Hour. This could work in two ways. Firstly English work such as reading to the class could feed back into the Literacy Hour — the opening page of a story could be the text for the day. Secondly the reverse could happen, so that work on a text in a Literacy Hour (e.g. a Big Book version of *The Hungry Giant*) could lead to drama and play in which both the plot and the language patterns can be explored and developed.

In the policy document the coordinator will have to state intentions and back them up with the reasons why it is important for children to experience certain activities each day at Key Stage 1. It might have been decided that every day children will sit down and share a Big Book reading. This is where focused, concentrated, specific teaching of reading skills can take place. Similarly at some point in each day the children will be expected to sit around an easel and watch closely while the teacher models writing, drawing on the children's knowledge and experience.

As already stated, some teachers can get very twitchy about feeling they are being told 'how' to teach, so somehow you have got to get across the understanding that such shared practices are for the benefit of the children and that there is still room for individuality. Sometimes conflict arises from unexpected quarters. A coordinator can go carefully through all these processes with the implementation of writing folders, only to have a teacher dig her heels in at the last moment and refuse to use them. If support from the headteacher is not forthcoming then the prospect of stalemate is high. Check and double check that you have the support of senior management before leading a major change or the consistency sought will not become reality. The coordinator needs to be able to stand up in front of staff and parents and say 'each child has a writing folder because . . .' and know that it is happening.

In time, the coordinator needs to take staff through each aspect of the English curriculum, emphasising teaching suggestions and learning outcomes at each stage. All areas of the curriculum are important, but at Key Stage 1 literacy acquisition has to be up there at the top. The effective literacy teacher uses and manipulates the curriculum to give every learning experience, in all subject areas, a literacy component. The Literacy Framework needs to be understood as well as simply implemented in order to get the best results.

You need to ensure that reading is approached in the same way from class to class. It is damaging for a child to go from an encouraging, supportive learning situation where sharing a book *with* a teacher is a treat, to a class where reading *to* the teacher takes on the feel of a test.

Through discussion, establish an agreement on how many times each week a child will read on a one-to-one basis with their teacher and other classroom helpers. Agree on the procedure for such reading sessions. Are you going to concentrate on quality time twice a week or little and often each day? For the beginning reader it is advisable to read the text with the child before the book is taken home, then the sharing time with the parent has the chance to be a positive experience. If you are going to use the bookmark system described in an earlier section, then everyone should follow the same practice. At all times build into your policy document the consistencies that will help the children.

Parents can best work with teachers for the good of their child if they too know what is expected. So, if the policy of the school is a belief in the importance of reading words in context, then you cannot allow one teacher to send words home in a box, to be learned before the child is permitted to read a book containing that vocabulary. If as a staff you value reading for meaning and pleasure, then don't allow some teachers to send a book home with the instruction to read specific pages. If a child is eager to read on, then let them.

The area of writing is a similar minefield. As coordinator you must ensure that everyone is aware of, and follows, the agreed process in the development of the child as a writer. Teachers must have the same *positive* approach to errors in the young writer's work. Mistakes must be seen as an important part in the learning cycle or how else will the child have the courage to experiment with and extend their use of words? However, the coordinator needs to emphasise that the mistakes the child makes must inform the direct teaching that takes place as a result of those errors. It would be as well to go through the stages of the writing process based on, for example the work of Donald Graves. Don't assume knowledge. Spell it out clearly, drawing the links with your own special situation.

Handwriting is an easier area and one where the emphasis needs to be put on teaching handwriting as a separate skill. Link it by all means with spelling patterns, but don't let it interfere with the creativity of thought processes when a child is composing.

A section on successful classrooms could be added. This might sound a bit silly, but some teachers honestly don't always know what success looks like. Teachers can very easily become isolated in their classrooms, repeating tried and tested methods year in and year out and unless there is a comfortable culture of peer observation some people can become entrenched. Let's take time to look at the qualities of successful literacy classrooms.

Successful literacy experiences

In successful learning experiences there is deep engagement and the children recognise the links in their learning, allowing evidence to show up later. Brian Cambourne (1988) points out that in successful literacy learning:

- activities are preceded by explicitly stated purposes so that the children know what they are doing and why they are doing it;
- they involve children in high degrees of social interaction and cognitive collaboration; they are structured, well planned, systematic, mindful and contextualised.

In successful literacy learning situations children and teachers have high expectations. 'Yes you are all going to become readers, but for some it will happen before others.' They are the classrooms where the teacher and children talk openly about this business of becoming a reader and writer; where children are taken on regular 'print walks' in order to focus their attention on how print works and where decoding and encoding print becomes the 'raison d'etre'.

In successful classrooms important things get done, not just children involved in activities to keep them busy and out of trouble. We have all seen children 'colouring' themselves into oblivion. Creative art work is great, but in some classrooms children seem to spend a high percentage of time in each task on activities not directly associated with the learning. Children should be engaged in important tasks that build on previous learning and extend, strengthen and embed the learning.

In successful literacy environments children are aware of time and deadlines. They don't waste time. Successful classrooms are efficient workplaces which are tidy and organised. Children know where to find things and don't waste time wandering around wondering where the pencil tub has been abandoned.

In successful literacy classrooms, children are involved in their own learning; they have a developed sense of ownership, are given responsibility and are trusted to make choices.

Compare this image of successful experiences with that extolled by the Literacy Framework; is there much difference? The Literacy Framework is pulling together good practice to try to encourage a real thrust for quality for children and a concerted approach by teachers.

Classroom organisation for the enhancement of literacy learning

If we are to develop a love of reading in these young children, then the book area of the classroom has to act like a magnet to pull the children into reading. The coordinator has to make teachers aware of the power of good display technique. Books need to be displayed with the cover showing. In bookshops, the current bestselling paperbacks, or those books the shop wants to promote, are displayed on rotating stands with their covers facing the browser. Hardbacks are often spread out on a large table. Encourage teachers to use the same strategies for promoting books in their classrooms. Get teachers to have a corner with wall-hanging racks where again books can be displayed with covers facing outwards.

Books need to be changed regularly and new ones introduced. How you do this will depend on the way you allocate books in your school. Let us illustrate this with reference to the practice in one school.

Here all the books are kept in a central library. Multiple copies of books that work well with children have been acquired. Teachers go to the library and take a selection of texts for their classrooms and some are put back each week and others taken out when the children visit the library. Even the youngest children become involved in the renewal process as they are asked to select those that everyone has enjoyed and can therefore be returned for other children to experience. Teachers are asked to have a wide selection of texts in their rooms including story books, factual texts of a level appropriate to the development of the children, poetry books, joke books, song books, information texts, picture dictionaries and so on.

A book area needs to be a comfortable place for children to sit and read — a carpet and a few cushions can create a cosy area. Make sure the cushion covers are removable and therefore washable, have you ever noticed how many classroom cushions appear to be health hazards. Similarly the carpets need to be cleaned regularly and thoroughly cleaned perhaps once a year. Emphasise the importance of training young children to take great care of books, encourage them to replace books carefully, especially in those white metal wall displays. Make sure the books are put back the right way up, with the front cover facing outwards. When this becomes an accepted concern from the early school years, then the habit will stick. If this is where the teachers will spend time reading with children then the chair the teacher uses must provide ease of vision over the whole classroom. It's no good if the book corner is situated behind a stockade of cupboards, for then the teacher will waste time bobbing up and down to see what is going on.

Teachers will need to decide whether they are going to have an area specifically for writing, or just an area where all the writing equipment is stored for easy access. This needs to include different types, shapes and colours of paper, pencils, pens and coloured crayons, scissors, glue, staplers and any other equipment necessary for publishing. For these very young children some ready-to-use, two or three page 'books' in a variety of sizes will be useful. Resources for spelling need to be at hand and clearly visible from where the children will be sitting to write. Lists of words with common patterns, family words, topic related vocabulary all need to be on hand as long as the children have helped to collect and compile those lists, otherwise they are just interior design.

If folders are to be used where will they be kept? Where will you locate a filing cabinet to hold the portfolios? All these issues need to be thought through. As coordinator you need to be there to suggest, assist, encourage and praise.

Time allocation

The amount of time that each child is involved in literacy activities and their variety, needs to be clearly spelled out. Statutory requirements come and go, but the thought of only one hour a day being devoted to literacy activities is alarming. Perhaps what we need at Key Stage 1 is the one hour a day of direct teaching, followed up by the majority of activities having a literacy component. When children are involved in mathematics they are often reading instructions, having to sort out exact meanings and understand the language of mathematics. Science activities require the development of specific vocabulary, detailed observation, problem solving, thinking, collaboration and written recording. There are few elements in the curriculum that don't lend themselves to a focus on speaking and listening, reading and writing.

Children's entitlement

Clear guidelines need to be developed within the school on the issue of entitlement. Teachers need to be encouraged to be vigilant in their observation of children who seem to be experiencing problems. By the second year of formal schooling decisions will need to be made as to whether this is a developmental lag or a specific learning difficulty. External advice might need to be sought. Similarly very able children need to be recognised so that their particular skills are not overlooked and disguised by the child, in an attempt to fit in with peers. Provision for the physically disadvantaged also needs attention. We need to be vigilant in observing children who don't appear to be seeing too well, perhaps the confused child has a hearing problem etc.

Left-handed children in this right-handed world can experience problems. They need to be seated on the left side of a group of two children. They ideally should have a seat that is higher than the norm because they need to raise their shoulder height to reach their arm around their writing. Left-handed children are often fidgets because they tend to sit with their weight on their right hip. A cushion to raise their height can cure all these oft undetected problems. There are some letters that left-handers form differently, e.g. the cross on the 't' and 'f'; as coordinator try to make sure that all staff are aware of such concerns.

The particular needs and rights of children for whom English is an additional language need to be addressed. You need a positive policy offering help and suggestions for teachers who are perhaps unused to dealing with a very different way of teaching. This is particularly important when the proportion of non-native speakers is dominant. For true immersion in the language to take place, children will need more English role models so ways to arrange this will have to be discussed.

Gender issues need to be addressed. Teachers should be aware of the amount of their time that is directed towards boys and girls. Research has found that boys tend to dominate and demand more teacher time. Displays need to be looked at to ensure that they portray a balance of male and female characters. Pay particular attention to the range of books within the classroom, do they reflect the interests of the whole class? Is there perhaps an over emphasis on the use of stories for beginning readers? Should we catalogue collections of factual texts that seem to have a greater appeal for boys?

In one school the coordinator had an appendix in the document where detailed check lists of common errors made by children with poor visual, auditory and orientational perception were a handy reference for the teacher.

Suggestions for displays

It is essential that the early years classroom is a particularly rich 'print environment'. The coordinator needs to encourage teachers to think clearly about what is to be written and where it is to be displayed.

For optimal effect, notices of importance need to be at eye height — child eye, not teacher eye. Anything to do with letter formation should be somewhere that the child can touch, tracing the shape with their finger rather than pencil. The notices displayed around the room need to be read frequently and changed regularly so that the environment is challenging as well as supportive. Displays should include questions to make children think. They can be interactive where a written response is invited. They have to show the children that reading has a real purpose in their lives and it is a good skill to acquire.

Links with the home

If there is to be a regular dialogue between home and school in the form of a diary or notebook, then the coordinator needs to establish a standard format and agreed involvement in order that parents experience consistency as their child moves from teacher to teacher. Agreement needs to be reached too on whether or not there are specific times when parents visit school or are they welcome at any time. Don't make a rod for your backs on this issue, time management is of great importance so a set time for informal visits is advisable. In the interest of security it is best that such visits should go via the school office.

For formal interview situations staff need to be clear on the specifics of literacy acquisition that they are going to discuss with the parents. If plenty of curriculum evenings are in place then there is no need for the teacher to explain 36 times how children are taught to write, parents can be referred to the next date and asked to attend. A two way partnership with involvement is what we are seeking.

Assessment and evaluation

In Chapter 8 we focus in detail on ways to monitor children's achievement. In your policy document you need to commit to print the decisions of the staff about the consistent ways you are going to monitor, moderate and evaluate the progress of all the pupils in the key stage.

Record keeping

Having collected all the data, how then are you to record so that teachers have ready access to the information? The future would seem to point to the use of IT to streamline, save space and avoid mountains of paper which inevitably gather dust and lose their freshness.

Resources

Clear statements on the use of resources need to be made to avoid unnecessary duplication and hoarding. We all have horror stories of characters who get to the stage of having padlocks on their cupboard doors for fear of anyone seeing what they have accumulated over the years. One memory is of a teacher who ordered no stationery items at all for the two years before she retired, she was somewhat like a camel surviving on stored energy.

Perhaps as a staff you will decide that individual requisitioning of equipment, other than small items, will cease. Everything then will be ordered with an overview of the needs of the whole English area. Items like Big Books are best kept in a central store but that doesn't mean that certain titles cannot be reserved for use with different age bands. Try to encourage the use of one Big Book per week in order to fully exploit the full teaching potential of the text and also decide on key texts that are to appear at particular stages of reading development. The interesting thing about modelling both reading and writing with young children is that they seem to take from the exercise that which is relevant to their immediate needs. For example in a shared reading of *Mrs Wishy Washy* one child might just be aware of the repetition in the text, while another is focusing on the use of punctuation. There is something to be gleaned by all in such shared sessions.

Recommended reading

Include, and keep updating a list of useful texts with a brief synopsis for teachers' reference. This list could be in two sections, essential reading and further reading. Make sure that these books are also available in the staff library.

English coordinator's job description

It is a good idea to include this, just so everyone knows exactly what your role is within the structure of the school and the extent of your responsibility.

Presenting the policy document

We must all have gone to work in schools where, on appointment, we are handed an enormous file including everything there is to be known about every detail of the school. It was often the property of the teacher you were replacing and as like as not was covered with rings of spilt coffee, ingrained with dust and the thousands of pages were dog eared and torn. Does anyone ever honestly read such documents? Certainly not in the weeks or days before

Don't be afraid to be creative, to look carefully at effective ways of influencing colleagues, to question the way 'it's always been done'. Do what you feel is best for your school.

appointment commences, nor in the weeks and months once you start, by which time you probably think you know what is going on, so there is no urgency to lug the file home. If you do, it will probably be put down and used as a door jam or flower press until you are asked to return it when you leave. If you did actually lift the cover and look inside it could well have been full of worthy suggestions of what should be done rather than an accurate account of what was being done. This might sound a rather jaundiced view but the point is that if we want teachers to read such documents then we have to make them user friendly, readable, accessible, jargon free and a true description of the practice in the school.

It is possible for each curriculum area in school to produce a booklet which is an accurate description of the good practice taking place in the school. The English document will be illustrated with examples of work from the children and will refer to specific examples of good practice. It should describe exactly the fundamental elements of literacy teaching that each teacher is to include in their planning for every school day. It should be produced in collaboration with the teachers and will become a working document that can be picked up and put down as the need arises. As new areas are addressed, so the document is added to or parts replaced. Plenty of copies can be made available and this well written, informative text can make staff both think and smile. The real appeal lies in the fact that it reads as a story of the school's development rather than as a dry set of principles and ideas. It is also a celebration of what has already been achieved and includes targets for the future. It is positive, full of enthusiasm and inspires the staff.

Not the end of the story

Eventually, the time will come when the major issues have been covered and for the time being the document is complete. This is a dangerous time when complacency can set in as people sit back on their laurels and relax. Yes, there is a need for consolidation, but there is also a need to keep abreast of new developments and to be vigilant in ensuring that what is written down is actually taking place. If you are not careful things can slip and people quietly return to their old ways because they feel the heat has been turned off.

The policy as a vehicle for staff development

If your policy is an accurate record of what is happening in English teaching in your school, then teachers with expertise will be acknowledged. We all have particular interests and someone who is a real whiz at, for example, teaching mathematics might have some hang ups about the strands of literacy teaching. Spelling is an issue in point. How many of us are confident spellers ourselves? How many teachers are basically frightened, through lack of understanding and low personal self esteem, of tackling the issue of spelling instruction? Many find it easier to give the children twenty words to learn each week and leave it at that. Teaching spelling creatively requires confidence and knowledge, so spell it out! How many teachers are addictive readers? It can be a bit difficult to promote the joy of reading in children if we do not enjoy it ourselves. There are those who excel in these areas and their skill needs to be shared with staff.

When a teacher shows a particular skill in an area try to arrange for others to be given free time to watch that teacher in action with the children. We can learn so much from each other and often a morning spent in another's classroom can give the observer the confidence to try for themselves. It is also terribly important to praise, most human beings respond to praise and strive to do well, but often the culture of the school ignores, or maybe just accepts excellence. Give credit where it is due. Another way of furthering professional development is to find the time yourself to go into classrooms and put the proposed system into action with the class teacher as an observer.

If funding is available then it is an excellent idea to get someone to come to your school to run an Inset day. There's nothing like an outside perception to raise issues and get staff talking. Try to press for a closure day, because twilight sessions after a busy school day have a limited appeal.

Individuals going on courses have a limited value unless a satisfactory way of sharing is devised. A report at the end of a staff meeting does little good. It's a bit like 'show and tell', a fairly useless waste of valuable time. What is more useful is asking the course participant to put one aspect of the course into practice and then report on the effect on the children's learning at a later date. This can be presented orally and then be written up and kept in a file for teacher reference.

Relationship to the School Development Plan

This can be a frustrating element when the coordinator is eager to get things moving fast in their curriculum area. Negotiation needs to be handled carefully, because if there is to be a school drive on 'history', then you need to find subtle ways to integrate literacy into the plan. It would be much better if schools decided to put the emphasis for the year on skills. For example, the focus could be developing problem-solving skills. You could then step in with strategies for collaborative group work involving children in the productive use of speech to develop thinking skills. The mathematics coordinator would also be happy developing lots of ways for children to apply mathematical meaning in real contexts. The science coordinator would also see relevance and press on with work on close observation, hypothesis forming etc. Everything would be linked, everyone would be actively involved, and no one would say, 'on your way, this is a history year'. The children would benefit from focused attention on the particular skill in learning. Otherwise there is the problem of children's interest being fixed into the curriculum area which matched a particular spurt in intellectual development.

Writing a good policy document takes you through the writing process from start to finish. You spend time mulling over the subject, thinking, observing, note taking, consulting. You draft, consult, redraft, edit, consult, publish and present. Your writing has a real purpose, real audience and gives everyone real experience of the process. When you come to the presentation stage don't just let it filter into the staff's awareness. Present it at a staff meeting, talk them through the process, give everyone a copy and perhaps provide tea and cakes by way of celebrating a shared achievement.

Chapter 7   Planning

The task of planning has assumed enormous proportions over the last ten years. Where teachers previously were encouraged to follow the excitement of children's learning, spot the development points, seize the moment and guide the children onto new dizzy heights, we are now expected to be less spontaneous. Teachers are expected to know the precise destination, work out the route, identify the best roads, seek diversions where necessary and avoid resting in lay-bys for fear that young people will be overtaken. As we venture towards Learning Goals for the Early Years which set standards which most children should reach by the end of the reception year, there is the very real concern that children beginning nursery will be rammed through a formalised learning experience which drills them in the outcomes expected at the end of the two-year cycle. This has immense dangers associated with it because, even at the end of the reception year, some children are 20 per cent younger than their colleagues and if we are drawn into comparisons in a negative way, the damage we do to young people at this tender age will be significant. We need to be very careful in the way we plan experience for children. If we deny the spontaneous; we deny learning. If we deny the opportunity to seize the moment; we deny teaching in its truest sense. Teachers need to be professionally critical about the tramlines upon which they are driven and need to be prepared to raise an eyebrow and

Planning breeds confidence.

a voice about the demands, not upon themselves, but on the youngsters. As a society, we are in danger of planning every step along the way for our children and the distance between potty training and A Levels will be little more than a series of rungs on a ladder. For many children though, the rungs on the ladder are not equidistant. They need the opportunity to put some rungs very close together so that they can take those small steps in learning and at other times the rungs can be set well apart so that they can take those great leaps of understanding.

Planning, though, breeds confidence. It breeds confidence in teachers in knowing what should be taught when and to whom and it breeds confidence in children in the belief that their teacher knows some routes through the learning maze. Children can identify when the teacher knows where they are going. They can sense the direction and are prepared to put themselves firmly in the teacher's hands. When the teacher is uncertain, wandering around looking for the next opening, the children are more likely to develop their own uncertainties and lack the enthusiasm for taking steps forward. Children do not have to know where they are going; they do need to know that the driver knows. They will enjoy the mystery tour of learning if the grown-up leading the way makes it exciting, even magical.

So, for the teacher the challenge is to plan an effective curriculum experience without the planning becoming overburdening. So many teachers have become so engulfed by planning procedures that they are overwhelmed by paper, need forklift trucks to take their planning files to school, and spend so much time planning that they have little time to prepare for the lessons that they have planned. This is not surprising, since in the last few years there have been so many changes to the education of young children that there have been few occasions upon which the teacher can be said to have been within a routine. Teachers, therefore, make charts and lists and notes and diagrams. They collect files, they cross-reference and they have meetings. The big challenge for teachers is to ensure their planning is worthwhile, provides a cost-effective use of time and makes an impact on children.

Where do we start?

As in planning for any subject, we start with the long term. We look at what needs to be taught over the period of Key Stage 1 and where children would be expected to be by the end of the two years. In English this is not too difficult since the National Curriculum provides the answer. Not only that, the Literacy Framework provides yet more answers! Given all the answers, it seems a shame that teachers are expected to sit down and create some more — especially when they are not sure what the question is! Given the Literacy Framework, the need to create long-term planning for the enactment of the Literacy Hour is much reduced. A three hour session for teachers involved in each year group within Key Stage 1 should be enough to help teachers to adapt the long term within the Framework to meet their needs. There would be a need for seeking out useful examples of text to be used, to try to relate the experiences that children need to meet with the local environment, for example. It would also be useful if, when pupils study different types of text, the materials used were collected from the local community. These could include items such as programmes for the local fete, adverts for local car boot sales, local election leaflets, postcards sold locally or car park tickets advertising local shops — all offer opportunities for added interest in the text through to word level work. Similarly with the National Curriculum for the wider area of English, it should be possible for teachers to manage the content into a plan for the two-year cycle. It is in taking this plan onto the next stage that the real detail starts to emerge.

Medium-term planning

Medium-term planning invites the opportunity to reposition the overall content within a sequence to suit the teacher and the children within a particular school. It is simply a case of taking all the pieces that need to be taught and putting them in an order that makes sense.

Within the literacy strategy the idea of working on units of work is promoted. Some of our learning comes in that 'drip,

drip, drip' of experience that we meet on a regular basis. Other learning experiences come about because we are able to do things in a block of time or in a block of experiences that run together. Some things are best learned when they make links with other areas of the curriculum and help children to see the way in which subjects work together. In planning it is useful to take forward the notion of continuous blocked and linked work through each half term of each school year.

The example on p. 130 offers one way of structuring an eight week programme of work to fit the National Literacy Strategy expectations. On the chart it is possible to see the work which is continuous within the four key areas of:

- phonics, spelling and vocabulary;
- grammar and punctuation;
- comprehension and composition;
- texts, in this case fiction and poetry.

By looking at the continuous work it is possible to tease out the elements of each focus area in order to ensure that children, over a period of eight weeks, experience that 'drip, drip, drip' that affects their:

- ability to punctuate;
- ability to spell;
- ability to use contextual clues to aid comprehension;
- ability to explain poems from other cultures.

Whilst this continuous work continues children can meet blocks of work at periods through each of the eight weeks. The chart tries to help teachers to plan a sequence of blocked activities, which covers the expectations of the literacy strategy. Hence, within comprehension and composition, the experiences of the children move from identification and discussion of favourite poems in week 1 through to writing their own poem from initial jottings in week 4. There is a gradual build up of expectation through the experience of the comprehension and composition block. A similar pattern is prepared for grammar and punctuation where children experience a gradually developing set of understandings related to speech which help to overcome some very difficult areas in children's learning.

NATIONAL LITERACY STRATEGY · Medium Term Planning Half Termly Planner · SCHOOL:

CLASS: · YEAR GROUP(S): 2 · YEAR: 19.99.... · TERM: Spring · 1ST HALF / 2ND HALF · TEACHER:

Texts: Fiction / Poetry

Range: Poems from other cultures. Poems with predictable and patterned language. Poems by significant children's poets. non fiction: Dictionaries, glossaries, indexes etc. i) Explanations.

Titles:

Phonics, Spelling and Vocabulary	Grammar and Punctuation	Comprehension and Composition	Wk
Continuous work Yr.1.T3 ① Read on sight high frequency words – abstract/abstract matched. Yr.2.T1 ⑥ words – high frequency. Yr1.T3 ④ Sight read 30 high frequency words. Yr.2.T1 ⑦ appendix list 1. Yr.2.T1 ① To secure understanding and use of. Yr.2.T1 ⑨ Long vowel + consonant. Yr.1.T3 ⑧ Long 'ed' 'ing' (tenses)	**Continuous work** ① To use awareness of grammar to decipher new or unfamiliar words. ② To read aloud with intonation and expression etc. ③ To re-read own writing to check for grammatical sense and accuracy.	**Continuous work** ② Produce simple flow charts 1) ① To reinforce / apply word level skills through shared / guided reading. ② To use phonological, contextual, grammatical, to look out, predict meanings etc. ③ through shared writing apply skills to spell words accurately.	Range of different poetry e.g:-	1
Blocked work ① ee and ea words * letts pg 13 ② oo (short), u (pull)	**Blocked work** T2 ④ Grammatical agreement in speech and writing e.g. I am I the children are. * own worksheet / letts pg 25	**Blocked Work** T2 ① Identify / discuss favourite poems / poetry use appropriate terms (verse, rhyme) ② comment on / recognise when reading aloud of poem is effective.		
① oi and a – e, ay words ② ar (car)	T2 ⑤ To use verb tenses accurately in speaking and writing, catch / caught, see / saw and to use past tense for narration, consistently. * letts pg 19. letts pg 7	⑤ To use structures from poem as a basis for writing. * Letts pg 10 – change words ⑥ Make class anthology of favourite poems.		2
① ie, i – e, igh, y. ② oi, oy		⑧ To read own poems aloud ① Identify / discuss patterns of rhythm / rhyme and other features of sound / line in different poems.		3
① oa, o – e, ow ② ow, ou (cow)	T2 To identify speech marks in reading etc. * letts pg 13. extension pg 23	⑥ As above. * write own poems from initial jottings / words.		4
① oo, u – e, ew, ue ② recap previous work.	T2 ⑦ To investigate and recognise a range of other ways to present texts e.g. speech bubbles, captions, * safety past, electricity.	⑥ Use dictionaries / glossaries to look words using initial letter. ⑪ Discuss definitions and explanations from above. Explore simple definitions ⑦ To use other information books using alphabetically ordered	Dictionaries, glossaries, Indexes, Directories, Encyclopedias.	5
		Make plans from topic dictionaries / glossaries. ⑥ Produce simple flow charts * Make glossary for l.h keepers books.	Flow charts	6
① Common spelling patterns for each of long vowel phonemes – identify, Yr.1.T1 blend in speech words. Yr.1.T3 ⑦ Learn to spell common regular words.			– Light House keepers books	7
Yr.2.T1 ⑨ learn to spell common irregular words (list 1) Yr.2.T1 ② Common spelling patterns for vowel phonemes. Identify, blend and segment. ④				8

* suggestions for tasks.

And so to the short term

Short-term planning occurs in different ways. The aim is to take the medium-term plan into a day-by-day analysis so that the content is sorted into manageable, bite-sized chunks. This can be done by looking at, in the case of the Literacy Hour, each section within the session and identifying what will be done in order to ensure that maximum use is made of the time available and to ensure that all phases of the hour are given equal status. On the chart on p. 132 you will see that the teacher sets objectives for the week, rather than for each session, and within each session tries to ensure that the objectives are met. Charts such as these are intended to get the bite-sized chunks into order so that there is a balance and a blend within the diet so that learning proteins are mixed with learning vegetables and learning fats in the right levels and proportions. Of course, the learning carbohydrate has to be there to keep the energy for living at a high enough rate. In the example the teacher has indicated where she will be engaged with the pupils ☺ and where the classroom assistant, Janet, will take a significant role 𝒥 .

Plans such as these are:
- easy to interpret;
- easy to check against objectives;
- easy to check for levels of challenge, variety and continuity within children's learning, along both the horizontal and vertical axes.

At the very planning stage, therefore, it is possible to ensure that curriculum coverage is maintained and in doing so a form of evaluation is already taking place.

Of course if these plans are done effectively and they work they can be simply filed away and returned to the next year. For some teachers this smacks of routine and going round and round the roundabout several times; for others the notion of a routine would be an absolute delight. It really is not necessary for teachers to do something new every time they begin a new piece of teaching. The children are new to the experience and the confidence in the teacher borne of having done the activity

W/E. 12/3

Week 3

Year Group 2   Text & Author: Assorted Texts.   Text type Poetry / Own narratives.

Objectives:
a) To read our poems aloud.
b) To identify and discuss patterns of rhythm & rhyme & other features of sound in poems.
c) To use verb tenses accurately & consistently - for narration eg past/present.
d) To look at common spelling patterns - identify, blend & segment
e) Learn to spell common regular & irregular words.

Ⓣ Teach
Ⓙ Joint

	Whole Class Shared Reading/Writing: Text level	Whole Class Shared Sentence/Word Level	Guided Reading/Writing	Independent Work: Individual/Pair/Group	Plenary	Resources
Mon	Look at own stories of "The Boy With Two Shadows". Look at key story points. Choose s. ones to correct together - what's missing?	Focus on words, sentences & punctuation in chosen story. Decide together what corrections need doing.	Red group: ☺ Group reading. Ⓣ G. writing : To work with those who have not finished Shadow stories.	Rosen: Blue, Green & Yellow group who have finished stories to look at Rhyming poem. Letts pg 27 & try own version. Ⓣ to introduce then with story work.	Choose completed Shadow 'story' to read out - use check list.	Own stories - Elliot's enlarged. Writing check list. Letts Bkt.
Tues	Look at Poems about 'Mums' - structure etc. Ideas for poem eg Helping, caring, Mum is... etc.	Rhyming word focus to help with poem writing. 'Ideas' brainstorm.	Guided Writing : Poem writing. Own attempts ☺ Ⓣ Group reading: Blue Group.	Green & Red Group. Writing poems - own attempts/models.	Choose s.o.'s attempt at poem writing.	Poetry on subject of 'Mums'. Letts Term 1 pg 8.
Wed	...Letts Term 2 pg 8 - Text. "Why do dogs chase cars?" Discuss what sort of text/story ... past tense.	Look at verb tense - Substitute present for past tense - which sounds right?	Group reading: ☺ Green group. Ⓣ Guided writing: Yellow group - Verb tense.	Blue & Red group - Verb tense - Sentence work - Choosing correct tense of verb to write in sentence.	Recap tenses. Choose some examples of sentence work completed - which tense is correct?	Letts Poster "why do dogs chase cars?"
Thurs	Phonics: The Big Phonic Book - AL Long 'i' vowel phonemes. Group ② Introduce 'ar' phoneme.	AL phonemes - (Look for long 'i' vowel spelling patterns. ie, i-e, igh, y) Note ar or action. group ② 'ar' words	Group reading: ☺ Yellow group + Shania Ben. Ⓣ To take phonic group ① - what words & explain task.	Blue & Green group - phonic follow up 'a' work. Red group: long 'i' vowel work follow up task.	Look at lists ie, i-e, igh or words. How many new and have we found?	Big Phonic Books. + Relevant games/ flip books.
Fri	Read & enjoy selection of poems seen so for eg Letts / Big Books/Own. Recap what we have learnt about poetry so for.	Prediction & substitution of words in text. Looking more closely at our poems.	Guided writing: ☺ Blue group. A Poem for Mum.	Green, Red & Yellow groups - copying out poems in best handwriting. Ⓣ - Giving help where needed.	Look at 'best' copies completed.	Big Books, Posters etc of Poems so for.

before will make it enjoyable. Naturally if children are in mixed age classes there needs to be some variation, but even a two-year cycle would create some routine that could be enjoyed by teachers and children alike.

And within the lesson . . . the very short term

So many teachers make such copious notes for lessons that it takes longer to write the notes than it does to teach the lesson. A plan for a lesson is for nobody other than the teacher and as such it needs to be a set of jottings, rough notes, scribbles . . . anything that helps the teacher to find their way through the next hour. It needs to be easy to refer to, quick to check and a useful *aide mémoire* so that in the busy life of the infant school classroom it is possible for the teacher to reflect upon her thinking, remind herself of what she meant and get on with it. It is like a shopping list, a recipe or a step-by-step guide for the neighbours who are looking after the house for a week while we are away. It needs to be easy to follow, easy to understand and easy to do!

In the example of a literacy lesson plan on p. 134 you can see that the teacher has made notes to herself about:

- what she is going to do;
- what she is trying to achieve;
- what she wants the children to know;
- who is doing what;
- how shall we use time.

She has also recorded which resources she needs so that in the busy day-to-day life of the classroom she can check she has got everything before she sets off on the journey through the hour. Too often teachers write down every single resource and treat themselves like amnesiacs — there is no need.

Literacy Lesson Plan

Text Level: *Phonic Big Books:*   *(Introduction for*
<u>Whole class shared reading</u> *"Long 'i' rhyme" pg 4.*   *Yellow & Red groups.*
Look for long 'i' vowel phonemes   *Revision for Blue &*
                                      Green groups)
<u>Blue & Green group only</u>: *Vowel phoneme 'ar' as in car*
- *Read "Mark the Shark"*   *'a' as in class.*

Sentence & word level

<u>Red & Yellow</u> *group to work with C.A. - Looking at different*
spellings of long 'i' vowel sounds : <u>y, igh, i-e & ie</u>.
Make appropriate lists ~ Go over independent tasks.

<u>Blue & Green group</u> *to work with me :- Introduce 'ar' vowel phoneme*
and "a" without the r ~ Make lists of words ~ Introduce tasks.

Independent & group activities

<u>Yellow group</u> : *Group guided reading with me :*

<u>Red group</u> : *Shared / guided writing with C.A.*
Using templates, finding words.
Activity sheet 6 if task completed.

<u>Green group</u> : *Activity sheet 17. + Word search if finished.*

<u>Blue group</u> : *6 'ar' sentences + "   " : "*

Plenary *Quick recap of phonemes learnt today :*

ie, y, igh, i-e and 'ar' & 'a'.
Read sentences written by children if time.

NOTES

<u>Resources</u> : *Big phonic books.*   *Blue English work books.*
               Photocopied activity sheets.   *Yellow group readers.*
Bag of 'ar'   *Templates for Red group.*
objects.   *Menu board set up for 'early finishers'.*

What about areas outside literacy?

Because literacy has assumed so much importance it is easy to think that English does not need to go through the same process. In many ways this is correct because teachers can spend so much time planning English when the aspects of English considered within the context of literacy are simply repeated. What is essential is that planning takes account of all aspects of English and, in this respect, it is important to plan speaking and listening opportunities. As has been already stated, speaking and listening form a vital part of the English curriculum. However, planning for development in this area is often very weak. There is an assumption that speaking and listening will happen, that teachers will make it happen and that children will do it. Unless the sessions are structured effectively there is a danger that children will wait forever for that spark of spontaneity and when it happens the teacher will be looking the other way teaching literacy and will miss it.

Speaking and listening need to inform all areas of the curriculum and as a school it is important to think through the basic skills that will be developed in relation to vocabulary development.

In many ways speaking and listening are the process of English and it is easy to neglect the planning element.

In planning for speaking and listening we need to identify teaching opportunities. At the long-term stage it is possible to provide a framework which offers a way in which staff can create opportunities for speaking and listening within the explicit National Literacy Framework for reading and writing.

Children need to:
■ have opportunities to speak and understand the notion of audience;
■ have a chance to listen and respond;
■ discuss and interact with each other;
■ engage in role play or drama.

The challenge at the long-term planning stage is to identify ways in which play opportunities can be used to develop speaking and listening and reading and writing opportunities, thereby ensuring that literacy is part of the bigger English field.

One important element of the teaching of speaking and listening relates to role play and this is an area in which schools need to take the opportunity to create really worthwhile and effective learning opportunities. For many children role play simply means going into a little plywood house, putting on the checked dressing gown, sometimes wearing a stethoscope and stirring pans very fast. Children know that you do this sort of thing while you are waiting for the teacher so that you can get on with some real work like reading, writing or number!

Half Term → Year Group & Objectives ↓	1	2	3	4	5	6
Speaking & Listening **Nursery** Writing	teddy bears picnic	shop	home	book setting	· to+ nnni petrol station · price/price	· guided tours museum · descriptions g artefact
Speaking & Listening **Reception** Writing	market	· costumed · convit/ banter cafe/fast food · menu · hit list	· waiter/pen servit · costume menu · price	· news agent · p ynt ar sy rt · poster	· dramatic recording book setting	
Speaking & Listening **Year 1** Writing	· explanation g an event doctor magic · persuption · promenent	library · persuading writing	· children in pairs shopping and discussing what they saw on TV. supermarket · adverts for promoting products	Children to present the weather forecast using correct language weather station · practise recording the weather on a chart	lighthouse	airport/station · tickets · baggage handling · travel tips
Speaking & Listening **Year 2** Writing	· role play drama actor, lighting TV studio · schedule · scripts	pet shop	travel agent · tickets · brochure · booking	garage	on the beach · postcards	· explanation g plant care garden centre · labels · instructions

Planning for the role play area.

True role play areas give children the opportunity to do exactly that — to play in different roles. Whilst they play in different roles they have an opportunity to experience different reading and writing activities with a real purpose and a real audience within the context of their imaginative play situation. Long-term planning can exist within any aspect of our classroom management and this is exactly the case in terms of role play.

The chart on p. 136 offers a starting point for the planning of role play areas in each of the six half terms within a year over the four years from nursery to Year 2. By varying the location children have an opportunity to engage in a range of play experiences. In the upper half of the box we can record the type of learning experience that the children will have within the context of speaking and listening. In the lower portion of each box we can record the type of reading and writing experience that can be provided to link with the role play area. If the whole staff, including classroom assistants and nursery nurses, are engaged in completing this sort of chart the opportunity for real dialogue about outcomes, purposes and audiences within the context of speaking and listening will provide real links with the literacy developments taking place elsewhere. The chart is simple to complete, but after a morning engaged in deep discussion about the value of play, will create valid learning chances for children for a period of four years. That's when long-term planning is worth it.

Part four Monitoring for quality

Chapter 8
Assessment

Chapter 9
Baseline assessment

Chapter 10
Evidence of achievement at
Key Stage 1

Assessment

Monitoring seems to be one of those words that has slid into prominence over the last decade. It is something that teachers have always done but it now has a hi-tech name and unnecessarily worrying implications for many teachers. What it means is simply looking at what we are doing and evaluating the effect.

Why do we do it?

Evaluating the effectiveness of what teachers do with children in classrooms should be an intrinsic part of the coordinator's role. Monitoring gives teachers:

- the means to improve and develop their teaching;
- the opportunity to document the children's progress;
- the chance to identify individual needs;
- an insight into children's strengths as well as their weaknesses;
- a means of gathering information for school records;
- the data to talk to parents about the specifics of their child's learning pattern.

What the children have learned tells us how successful the teachers have or haven't been in meeting their pupils' particular needs and situation. The evaluations they make should then influence the future planning and approach they take to maximise the benefit to the children in their care. The reason for doing it is 'the child'. The child's needs are central to everything we do.

So often in schools, assessment is seen as a tedious activity, a statutory requirement which is done because it has to be done. It is often left until the last possible moment, just before reports have to be written or parent interviews carried out. Whether or not an *evaluation* is ever made of the assessment, and action taken, is debatable. What should be happening is that teachers monitor children's achievements in a continuous form of data collection upon which they evaluate and make judgments on the effectiveness of the teaching and learning situation. So often, teachers say, 'yes we know this, but how can we find the time to do everything?' This is where we need to turn to those who have had the luxury to research and spend time concentrating on one particular area at a time. Cambourne and Turbill (1997) set out four criteria for effective assessment and evaluation which clarify and help the teacher.

1   Assessment and evaluation must result in optimal learning for all.
2   Assessment and evaluation must inform, support and justify teacher decision making.
3   Assessment and evaluation practices must reflect the theories of language learning and literacy learning which guide our teaching.
4   The findings which result from our assessment and evaluation practices must be accurate, valid, reliable and be perceived to be rigorous by all who use them.

A far cry from the 'board game' mentality of the tick sheet of achievements: Can the child do x,y,z? If the answer is yes move on, if no, then go back to the beginning, do not pass Go, do not pick up any encouragement, start again on exactly the same process. Can the child recognise and say the sounds of the 26 letters in the alphabet? If yes, put a tick in the appropriate box . . . but . . . can the children apply this knowledge in their own writing? . . . That is what we really need to know and is far removed from the mountain of tick sheets that accompanied each child as they staggered through the journey of titles to find their way to the end of the reading scheme. Those lists of books told us nothing about the reader's

As English coordinators we do not want to perpetuate that kind of 'record keeping' for that's all it was, a record. We want to know more about what children can do in the classroom situation, on their own and in collaboration with others. We need an insight into their potential.

involvement with the text, level of understanding, reading strategies for unknown words, fluency, accuracy or pleasure, they just told us which books the children had been exposed to. The implication for the child was that reading was a race, read a book, move to the next title, on to the next colour band, never revisit a favourite, slog on through and then . . . that's it . . . made it . . . never read for pleasure . . . because the experience was so boringly tedious and often cripplingly painful.

What do the children need from this whole business of assessment? Does anyone ever tell them what is going on? Children, even very young ones, need to be aware of, and have the chance to recognise and celebrate their own progress. We must give them the opportunity to establish a high self estimation of themselves as learners. They have the right to strive to achieve and recognise their best work. These young active learners can be involved not only in the process, but also in the progress of their own learning.

When to do assessment

Many teachers say that they are asked to do so much assessment that the time they have for teaching is getting less and less. This will be so if assessment is viewed as an extra task. If, you, as coordinator, can ensure that it is seen as an everyday part of the teaching programme then it does not pose so great a threat. Also, if the teachers are actually doing something with the evidence they collect then the exercise assumes a positive benefit for everyone, especially the children. The class teachers are then actively taking responsibility for what happens in the classroom rather than being accountable. This issue is further discussed by Helen Woodward (1993) in her text on *Negotiated Evaluation*. She refers to the importance of time management in the classroom and suggests that if teachers do not manage their time well, then evaluation procedures will not be productive. She refers to 'positive' and 'negative' classroom time. The collection and analysis of data, from a variety of sources and perspectives which is helpful in decision making about the children's learning and future planning, puts the teacher in 'positive' time. Collecting data in a rush that you are not going to do anything with, puts you in 'negative' time. Over the years more and more responsibilities have been put on teachers and negative time seems to have overtaken positive. This needs to be adjusted for the good of everyone.

Assessment opportunities

We need to begin by considering assessment opportunities, then strategies. We can consider the chances for assessment in the whole class element of the Literacy Hour, during the shared read or write, or in the plenary. The following examples show some of the techniques that can be used:

- orally given tests of set of questions every two weeks with mixed questions, followed by class discussion;
- plan for one or two days of assessment activities or written tasks at the end of each half term — combine with recorded work over previous six weeks to identify development and any misconceptions;
- activities or tests which are given before and after a new topic is introduced, to see what is known beforehand, and then to check on progress (concept or mental mapping);
- games and activities which assess the general knowledge and understanding in the class;
- observational assessments and questioning are made without undue distraction — target group within whole class activity, notes made by teacher or classroom support;
- build into the planning the vocabulary to be used and the questions you expect to ask — use of specific questions to certain children;
- build up a store of questions to extend the children's thinking — keep changing the ways that questions are asked to develop fluency in technical language — aimed at a particular module 1 topic;
- consider the simplifications and extensions of resources/activities used, and easier and harder questions so children can be included at their own level;
- be clear about the nature of, and progression in, the ideas and skills that are being taught in either a particular lesson or group of lessons (when does the assessment come?).

Assessment areas within the Literacy Hour

Assessment strategy	Opportunities
Skills checklist — related to teaching and learning (collaborative group work)	
Miscue analysis — techniques used, specific cues targeted	
Observation grid — context provided for observation of specific knowledge, skills and understanding	
Concept mapping — establishing what children know and understand	
Criterion referenced tasks set during independent activities	
Opportunities for self assessment — learning outcomes shared with children	
Targeted questions — checking understanding/thinking of children at different stages in the session	
Planned opportunities for discussion about the learning between teacher/pupil and pupil/pupil	
Building a personal portfolio or album of literacy achievement	

Such activities provide the opportunities for assessment and can easily be slotted into the Literacy Hour assessment chart above. Each group of children will vary so the opportunities will be wide-ranging. The strategies are likely to be relevant across the key stage.

Assessment during the Literacy Hour

The following range of strategies are offered as suggestions for assessment during whole class, individual and group time.

Whole class

All children to be individually given a copy of shared text. Children can then highlight sections of the text, with word or sentence level activities. (Note — shared read doesn't always have to be on the carpet.)

Ongoing assessment — focus upon individual children or have target groups. Accompanying each unit of study could be a set of questions which you use over a period of time to assess what is being learnt. Specific questions can be used with certain children i.e. 'differentiate' with the type of questions used.

Be clear about the ideas and skills that are being taught either in a lesson or series of lessons — build into planning any questions you are to use or vocabulary you intend to introduce.

Use class discussion to respond immediately to misunderstandings or something that needs reinforcing. More intensive support could be provided during the independent task time.

Share the learning objectives at the beginning of the week. Target certain children each day to check if the objectives have been met. (More able children could be assessed at the start of the week with strugglers towards the end.) Celebrate children's achievements by having a class chart which the children can mark at the end of the session. One such chart can be seen on page 149.

Classroom assistant may be used to complete an observation grid during the shared read and following activities. Grids with up to three learning objectives can also be used by the teacher during the plenary.

Written task may be given to the children (and explained during the shared write session) which links the reading to the writing and illustrates an assessable 'outcome' for the end of a unit of work. Consideration needs to be given to the approach used by the teacher in marking the work.

Concept maps could be drawn both at the beginning and end of a unit of work to show what is initially understood by the child and the achievement at the end. Children should be encouraged to share what they have learnt during the plenary.

Shared write — read to a certain point in the script where two characters are about to talk. Stop and ask children to discuss what the following dialogue might be. Take some ideas and model how they might turn their ideas into a simple playscript with a stage direction. Set them the task of writing their own playscript during the group work. Each child needs to produce their own piece of work. This could be included in a personal portfolio and marking matched to writing targets.

During the plenary:

■ target group to read out their dialogue (having explained that they will be chosen to do so at the start of the session). Use observation grid to assess presentation skills. (Grid is shown below.)

■ whole class can do a concept map about what they know about playscripts and then be encouraged to talk about what they have learnt.

Activity 7

Example using 'play scripts' — Year 3

Section of playscript to be used individually — individual children chosen to read. A grid, like the one below, can be used to record play reading performance.

Focus on extract from play. Word level activity, i.e. can children underline prefixes? Look for verbs that can be changed into their opposite meaning using the prefixes un-, dis-. Encourage children to mark the text. Which verbs couldn't we change? Can more able children suggest an alternative verb that has a prefix? i.e. leaves changes to *disappears*, puzzled changes to *unsure*.

Further set of questions which could be used:

■ Can you think of two things that make a play script different from a story book?
■ Can you tell me what we include in the stage directions?
■ Who are the main characters in the play? How do we know this?
■ What does dialogue mean?

The above can be used during the shared write session.

Play reading performance **Date** ....

Name → Focus ↓						
Fluency ■ intonation ■ rhythm						
Effectiveness ■ pronunciation ■ diction ■ clarity ■ audibility						
Non-verbal language ■ facial expression						

Activity 8

Using poems with familiar settings — Year 2

Whole class: shared read Introduce book, what type of book is it, how can you tell, how are poems different from a story?

Poem read to children. Keep up rhythm of text as you read so that children can predict what is coming next and join in with poem and hear intonation.

Individual children chosen to re-read — again, use a grid like the one on p. 147 to record reading behaviour — skills children are using (i.e. does child use a variety of approaches to word recognition).

Questions used to encourage literary response from children. (p. 149)
1   What do you think the poem is about?
2   Can you visualise parts of the poem?
3   Can you tell me something about how it is written?
4   What do you notice about the words that rhyme?

Word level Investigate and classify words with same sound but different spellings;
■ children highlight words that rhyme — model process — scribe on board.

Model to children how to sort words into those that: sound the same; same spelling at the end and those that sound the same; not the same spelling at the end.

Children targeted individually with pair of words to sort and the rest of the class has to decide whether they are right or not.

Tasks
Group 1: Assessment of reading behaviour, use of rhyming words.
Children read sentences and complete them with a given rhyming word.

Group 2: Assessment of reading behaviour, inventing own rhymes.
Children read sentences and invent own rhyming word.

Group 3: Assessment of how children work in a group — use of grid.
Using 'The Owl and the Pussycat' — children underline words that rhyme, spot patterns in poem.

Plenary Target group 2 (having explained that they will be chosen to do so at the start of the session).
Use observation grid to assess presentation skills. (p. 147)

Some further ideas to stimulate response to the poem

Are there any parts of the poem you remember? Why?

If you close your eyes and think about the poem, what are the pictures in your mind?

What does the poem make you feel, think about?

Are there any patterns in the poem?

Can you tell me something about how it is written?

What do you notice about the words that rhyme?

I can…

Focus	Name					
I can contribute to whole class discussion						
I know what dialogue is						
I can think of a prefix						
I can read with intonation						

An example of an achievement chart to be filled in by each child

Involving pupils in their learning

Pupils need to be given opportunities to make judgments about their learning and have time to reflect upon it. For example, children can have a shared responsibility for the contents of their individual portfolios. The evidence collected will demonstrate success in both the teacher's and child's eye.

The class teachers identify at least five key learning outcomes for every half term. These are shared at the beginning of the term with the whole class so that the children are aware of the targeted learning outcomes.

Children can also be given an opportunity to be involved in the process of setting targets and should then be able to articulate what they feel they have achieved as a class. Children have to be able to gain evidence for the achievement and say when they did the work. Teachers will need to think through this in more detail in terms of what is practical and possible in a class of 35 children.

Performance Indicators in Primary Schools: PIPS

These provide teachers with an ideal opportunity to target their teaching to the needs of their class. They identify the skills children need to develop or already possess. They also enable teachers to communicate with parents about a child's individual capability — identifying the strengths of child and highlighting possible areas for parents to work with. (Teachers need to be selective with parents about what they share.) Furthermore, PIPS allow the teacher to identify commonalities in the class and can be used to target teaching.

To summarize

Decision about assessment must address the following:

1 children's understanding of the content;
2 children's attitudes or behaviours;
3 children's thinking processes — checklist for guiding observations and for focusing teachers' questions in talking with individual children;
4 skills — record of reading-like behaviour;
5 self-assessment.

Chapter 9   Baseline assessment

Getting the baseline and setting the target

Over the last few years schools have been encouraged to use quantifiable data, to a much greater extent than previously, when trying to judge whether they are performing well. The truth is that data, figures, percentages and proportions, targets, outputs and figures make no difference at all when used on their own. However, when used together in order to inform practice and to change approaches to teaching for the better, all of these pieces of data can be of benefit. Much documentation is now being produced about how schools can move practice forward through using data and, from many sources, schools are being helped to understand their own performance by using some fairly refined procedures to know their baseline and establish targets within, particularly, the core subjects.

Many LEAs have baseline assessment procedures which are in place for all their schools. Many LEAs also provide a service whereby they analyse statistical evidence and provide their schools with a sophisticated analysis. This includes a notion of bench marking and target setting to match the school with 'similar' ones elsewhere in the authority. The PIPS (Performance Indicators in Primary School) development is used across the country by different LEAs and is becoming a growing source of information about the attainment and progress of children at all levels. The gradually accumulating bank of data within the PIPS organisation is helping us to understand more and more about the impact that schools make and the way in which different schools add different values to pupil development.

Many schools, many teachers, many coordinators and many heads are worried about the development of statistical analysis and the complexities of using data to establish needs and performance targets for schools. However, if such developments allow us to understand what needs to be done and the effects of our efforts, put alongside other ways of monitoring and reviewing, such pieces of information are valuable to us.

A coordinator, therefore, needs to know how work in establishing baselines or targets fits in with the overall school policy. If the school uses the LEA system or the PIPS procedures in order to measure improvement then simply applying this is the way forward. However, having begun the way forward it is important to take the necessary steps and react to the data provided by addressing issues of teaching practices. It might be useful to consider ways in which the coordinator of English can look 'below the surface' of the data to make sense of information on offer.

Looking at baselines . . . starting points

Looking at a batch of scores is only half the picture; analysing the batch is often more interesting and more helpful. The diagram below shows pupil performance on some very simple tasks upon leaving Reception and the performance is represented in 'Box and Whisker' diagrams. Each child is represented by a circle and it is possible to put a box around the main block of pupils based on the medium score for the class.

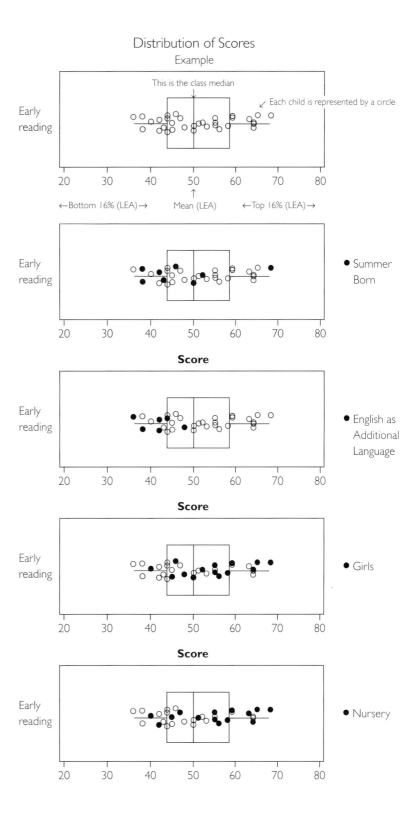

Distribution of Scores

From this box we are able to see where the children fall in terms of their performance within the school, but also within the LEA. In terms of reading it is then possible to look at where different individuals are to be found within the distribution of schools. So if we look at the early reading we can see that, in general, those children who went to nursery performed better than those children who did not. Those children who are girls perform considerably better than those children who are boys. Those children with English as an additional language perform significantly worse than those children who are naturally English speaking and those children who are summer born, that is later birthdays during the year, generally perform significantly worse than those born earlier. However, one summer born is in front of everybody in the class just to disprove the rule. This sort of information helps us to establish how teaching can be arranged in Year 1 and 2.

For instance:

■ we might need to target pupils who have English as an additional language to encourage them to make sufficient progress;
■ we may need to look at the materials given to boys to ensure that it attracts their interests and encourages the right attitudes so that they do not become left behind by the girls;
■ we might need to look at children who did not have nursery experience and see whether we can provide the range of learning activities necessary, not just within English, but in other aspects of the curriculum which will enhance their opportunities within reading over time.

Such possibilities emerge from careful analysis of baseline information.

Handling data at Year 2

An example of how analysis of PIPS results can be used is shown on p. 155 through highlighting issues and possible courses of action.

1 Several identified pupils are making less progress than expected in some or all subjects — some of whom were previously unknown cases.

Questions/lines of enquiry: Why is this? Do we need to demand more of these pupils or are we failing to motivate them sufficiently? Do we need to place these pupils on our Special Educational Needs register?

Conclusions to date: Each class teacher concerned has agreed to examine existing practices to seek a potential solution to the problem.

2 The children in one Year 2 class have made significantly greater progress in reading and in mathematics than the children in a parallel class.

Questions/lines of enquiry: Why is this? Is one teacher adopting practices which are more effective in producing results or are there other explanations for this?

Conclusions to date: Both teachers to investigate possible reasons for this including reporting on their respective classroom practices with a view to seeking answers and making recommendations for future practices.

The value of the information at baseline and at Year 2 level is that it helps us to think again about the practice in classrooms and makes us ask the questions which will improve opportunities for children.

Target setting fulfils the same function. Whilst at the surface level target setting involves looking at data, looking at the expected outcomes set by the government at Year 6 and working out how many children need to be able to clear a certain level each year, the targets can only be achieved if we adapt practice in the classroom to ensure that we make a difference. Most LEAs now provide information for teachers on how to set targets and once this process has been accomplished it is relatively easy to do it year on year.

Target setting using SAT results

The following graphs (pp. 156–7) show some of one school's results from KS1 for 1997 statutory assessments. They were compared with national (1997) figures. For example, the school found that they had no children achieving level 3 and that within level 2 any gradings were weighted towards 2c. They decided that they would have to set targets to raise attainment gradually, with some children achieving level 3, and more at 2b/2a. Compare the school's results against the national figures for writing and spelling.

Suggestion

What targets would you set for this year and next? (Obviously then you would have to consider the particular circumstances in the school to work out a plan to achieve these targets.)

Reading Comprehension Test (percentage at each level)

	School '97	National '97	School targets '98	School targets '99
2c	27	17 ⎫		
2b	9	17 ⎬ 48		
2a	18	14 ⎭		
3	0	26		

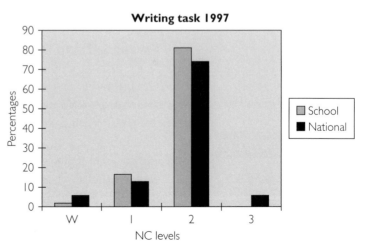

Writing Task

	School '97	National '97	School targets '98	School targets '99
Working towards	2	6		
level 1	17	13		
level 2	81	74		
level 3	0	6		

Writing task 1997

Spelling Test

	School '97	National '97	School targets '98	School targets '99
level 2	39	47		
level 3	7	14		

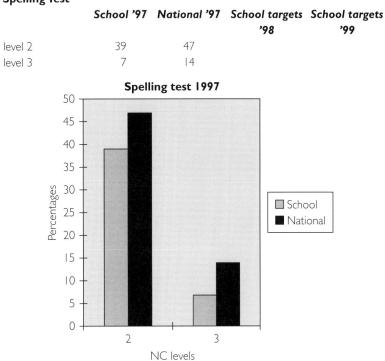

The following table shows another school's analysis of boy/girl results.

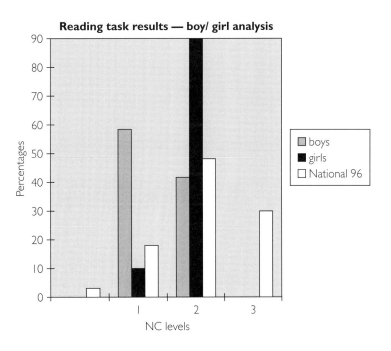

Of course the problem with the targets is that, for many schools, the input is not the same as the output, seven, three or four years later. For some schools the mobility of pupils means that they are dealing with very different children leaving from those that began this process of schooling some years earlier. Indeed, such reliance on figures in many cases fails to take account of the nature of schooling and shows a lack of awareness of anything other than the stereotypical childhood where a little boy or girl sets off to reception and stays in the school until they leave at Year 6. For many schools there can be inward and outward transfer of over 50 per cent of pupils during the primary phase and for some it is much greater than this. Therefore, target setting becomes a rather imprecise activity.

A further complication relates to the problem of increasing output beyond 'near maximum'. Once the school gets near to its target it is relatively difficult to raise performance even by 1 per cent over a year. Whereas, in business, targets can be raised by increasing the workforce, more efficient machinery, laying off the workforce, cheaper raw materials, schools essentially have to deal with the same background structures over long periods of time. Dramatic increases in performance therefore, will be difficult to achieve after say two successful years.

For coordinators of English, however, the task remains the same. The challenge of increasing the children's attainment over time and one way, but only one way, of achieving this is by projecting targets and considering ways forward. This can be done by using a relatively simple chart such as the one shown on p. 159 and offering targets and measuring progress. The principle of measuring a baseline simply continues each year throughout the age group as does the principle of measuring against targets achieved.

Target Setting — example — KS1 English — using NLP model and success criteria drawn from the Framework				
Standards at September 1998	Projected Target July 2000	Success Criteria: Key NLS objectives to be achieved	Progress at July 1999	Standards achieved July 2000
30% children L2 in reading	Reduce to 10% (20% 1999, 10% 2000)	Children make effective use of varied reading cues for prediction and tackling unfamiliar words. Pupils readily employ strategies for self-correction.		
40% children L2 in writing	Reduce to 20% (30% 1999, 20% 2000)	Children use phonic strategies for word-building as well as other sources e.g. word-blanks, dictionaries. Able to proof-read and independently self correct.		

Missing from this chart is a column which says, 'action to be taken'. This could be inserted next to the 'Success Criteria' column. However, the action to be taken should be clearly understood by all staff involved and may be extended to parents and children. Too often schools stop at setting the targets and then expect them to be reached. Essential to the achievement of targets is a clear understanding by everyone about the processes necessary to achieve them. In the end, all of the work on baseline assessment and target setting comes back to efficient, effective and worthwhile teaching strategies. Targets will only be achieved if people are doing their utmost to put into practice the very best teaching opportunities for children.

Chapter 10

Evidence of achievement at Key Stage 1

Children's achievements in reading

English coordinators need to start by looking at the ways we 'measure' reading achievement and consider the variety of valid assessment strategies open to them. These should be ways of discovering what the child can do, but more often than not they tell us what the child can't do. They don't necessarily tell us about motivation, attitude and personal growth towards becoming a lifelong reader.

Let's begin with the standardised tests of 'reading age' because one suspects they lurk in the cupboards of many schools and creep out, as much to reassure the teachers as to test the children. Think back to Part 1 when we referred to a text on the strategies used in the implementation of change: 'People tend to stick with what they know as a template for future decisions.' Parents also are used to the concept of their child having a 'reading age' and it tends to be a question that is asked, so teachers administer the tests to keep everyone happy, except perhaps the children.

Standardised tests

Standardised tests give us the chance to compare children against the average attainment of a very large number of

If you have a 'reading age', could you have a 'reading birthday' too? Presents to be in the form of books of course.

children of the same chronological age. There are usually two kinds, norm referenced and criterion referenced tests. Norm tests do not give us any information that can be used diagnostically. They just give us that 'reading age'. A criterion referenced test gives us an indication as to how far a reader has got in acquiring a set of stated skills.

If they are done as part of a series of assessment methods then they have a place as a back up in the overall picture. If, however, the children are marched to the headteacher's office twice a year to be tested, then their value is questionable. What tends to happen in such situations is that children and teachers progress happily along the set approach until about four weeks before the test date and then panic sets in and suddenly children are bombarded with flash cards that are about as useful to a child used to words in context as flash floods are to water retention. An anecdote at this point and a sobering thought is of a mother who got hold of a reading test and 'taught' her child to recognise enough of the words to gain a score well in advance of his chronological age. The teacher knew that the child couldn't read such words in context and asked him how he knew the words. With the innocence of youth he spilled the beans. Preparation for tests is not uncommon amongst teachers either. Pre-test stress affects teachers, parents and children and the higher the level of frustration the more likelihood there is that people will break the rules. Tests that are created with the best of intentions often have an effect that was far from the vision of the designers.

 Striving to do better oft we mar what's well.

Shakespeare, *King Lear*

Standardised reading tests originated in the 1940s before the surge in reading research. They were not designed to take into account all that we now understand about the reading process. In more recent times alternative methods have been devised.

Alternative methods of testing reading ability

Miscue analysis was first introduced by Goodman in the 1970s. It involves the child reading a text while the teacher notes any errors or miscues. By its very nature it requires the text to be stretching for the reader because the child is expected to miscue. It pays attention to syntactic and semantic cueing systems. At the end, the reader is asked to retell the story after the reading either orally or in the written form.

Running records is a procedure devised by Marie Clay in the 1980s that features in her reading recovery programme. What you do is to type the text of a number of pages of a variety of books found in your classroom and, at regular intervals, whilst the child reads the book you note the oral performance by highlighting any variation in the child's reading and the words in the text. Note omissions and strategies for dealing with unknown words. Special attention is paid to strategies the child uses to keep the meaning of the text. This is a simple resource to build up and can be done with material from a structured scheme or your own use of good books that help children become readers. Running records are the assessment method favoured by the Standard Assessment Task writers and are therefore familiar to most teachers.

Cloze analysis would probably be more suitable for more mature children, but the particularly gifted child might be given such a test to determine specific strategies being employed. Words are deleted from a text with the specific purpose of examining the reader's strategies for selecting a word to fit the gap. The reader's substitutions are analysed with reference to linguistic knowledge, knowledge of the story line, scanning techniques etc.

Retelling is a more recent procedure initiated by Brown and Cambourne, the emphasis being on getting meaning from texts. This would concentrate the reader on specific skills to highlight the main features of the plot, characters etc. This is particularly relevant when children are engaged in regular silent reading.

Observations and anecdotal notes The attitude and pleasure a child takes in reading is now considered to be as great an indicator of future success as skills for decoding. We must all have come across children at the top end of the primary school who can read with efficiency but no enthusiasm. If they take this lack of interest with them to secondary school, where their personal reading is perhaps not monitored so closely, then they can become lost readers. Enjoyment and interest in reading are vital.

If you decide that teachers are going to use *observation* as an indicator of achievement, what should you encourage teachers to focus upon? Observational notes are a useful reference for the class teacher but do not in general serve as a useful indicator for the next teacher, unless they address a set of mutually agreed criteria. It could be that you have a team of teachers in your school who work so closely together and value each other's judgements to such an extent that comments like 'Jan. 15th. He's taken off,' have a mutually understood meaning. However, for purposes of moderation, certain agreed criteria are advisable. Learning to closely observe children, knowing what to look for and having a means to record those observations are skills that initially need to be taught. If you are going to put a heavy reliance on observation in your school, then the observation has to be good. Not all teachers are confident so the coordinator will need to offer help and support.

As a staff, sit down and draw up a list of key points that suit the children and also tie in with the range of reading experience, the key skills and the language study requirements of the National Curriculum. Here are some suggestions gleaned from a number of schools. The important point is that they must match the needs of the children in your school and take into account background, culture and the resources of the school.

The beginning reader

At storytime:

- Does the child enjoy storytime?
- Does the child listen with concentration for more than five minutes?
- Does the child interact with the story by telling incidents that are related to his life?
- Can the child retell the story sometime later?
- Can the child recall particular characters and incidents?

When choosing a book:

- Does the child take time to select a book or just grab the first one to come to hand?
- Does the child search for a favourite book?
- Does the child display reader like behaviour, i.e. holding the book the right way up, turning the pages from the beginning to the end?
- Does the child spend time closely observing the pictures?
- Does the child choose books as a free choice?

When reading with the teacher:

- Does the child willingly share a book with an adult?
- Does the child 'hum along' when being read to?
- Does the child attempt to join in with the repeated line in the text?
- Does the child predict what is coming next?
- Does the child use the pictures to gain meaning?
- Does the child exhibit that 'stillness' of concentration that so often precedes reading starting?

When reading at home:

- Does the parent comment on the books that go home?
- Is the child encouraged to bring favourite books to school?
- Is the parent aware of the approach to reading used at the school?

The emerging reader

At storytime:

- Does the child recommend books to share with the class?
- Does the child anticipate and join in with the reading?
- Does the child search for patterns and carefully observe print during shared 'Big Book' readings?

When choosing books:

- Does the child browse and read some of the text before selecting?
- Does the child have favourite authors?
- Does the child stick to the safe and familiar?
- Is the child willing to attempt more complex books?

When reading with the teacher:

- Does the child show willingness to share a book?
- Does the child have a developing sight knowledge of words?
- Can the child distinguish known patterns in words to help break the word into syllables?
- Does the child use onset and rhyme to aid his reading?
- Does the child use alliteration and rhyme to help with the reading of unknown words?
- Does the child use context and prediction through a search for meaning or is he an 'individual word reader'?
- Does the child have a positive attitude towards trying to work out how to read an unknown word?

When reading at home:

- Is the parent involved in a dialogue about the child's progress?
- Does the parent employ the same strategies of reading support as you give at school?
- Is the parent anxious about the child's progress?

There are many, many more ideas you could include. As coordinator, initiate discussion as a staff for this gives ownership and ownership leads to action.

It is important to emphasize that observation should not take place at a fixed time but as a continuing process. The National Literacy Framework strongly advocates using guided reading sessions for this purpose. A notebook to jot down words and phrases to be transferred from time to time into the child's development file would be a good routine to suggest that teachers establish. Some teachers prefer to fix five or six children in their minds for a week, but it should be noted that this causes problems if others are having periods of tremendous progress. Common sense is called for on the part of the coordinator to sort these things out. Certainly with reading, having a notebook handy whilst teachers are sharing a book with a child gives the opportunity to record important developments.

In all of these alternative assessment procedures the coordinator must stress that the emphasis should be on what the child can do, not on what he or she cannot do. The procedures give the teacher an indication of progress and useful information can be acquired about the child's reading behaviour, rather than a focus on a fixed ability level which the standardised reading tests claim to give us.

It is also important that the methods of assessment reflect the philosophy of the school towards literacy acquisition. If you believe in the importance of reading for meaning then using a list of decontextualised words to test sight recognition ability serves little purpose and only frightens the child, who knows he is being tested.

This brings into question the whole business of children being assessed in unfamiliar settings. Being taken from the classroom one or two at a time to read a story to an unfamiliar teacher is not a true test of what the child can achieve and the validity therefore is questionable. As coordinator you will have to face this common practice and take a firm stand for what you believe to be in the children's best interest. Most coordinators would agree that if we are to gain a true picture of the child then a variety of procedures must be used.

Children's achievements in writing

As a school you need to have clearly defined beliefs about what you value in a developing writer and as coordinator you will have to instigate such discussion.

The assessment of the child's ability to express himself in the written word is perhaps not as contentious as achievements in reading. The National Curriculum guidelines emphasise the importance of purpose, process and audience. It encourages the pupils' 'early experiments and independent attempts at communicating in writing'. It encourages a collaborative, consultative approach to the teacher's involvement with the child and her/his writing in order to build confidence, independence and knowledge. We are encouraged to make children aware of the conventions of punctuation and a knowledge of the way spelling works. On the subject of handwriting children are to be taught to form their letters correctly and to develop a legible style. What we are being asked to do at Key Stage 1 is to lay firm solid foundations for future growth and to put the scaffolding in place to support the child throughout his school life.

- Do you all share the same understanding about the way children become writers and the process that they should follow?
- Do all the classrooms reflect that belief?
- How can we help each other to develop consistency for the benefit of the children?

One aspect that particularly pertains to assessing achievement in writing is the fact that when we look at a child's writing there are two distinct areas to focus upon. There is 'the writer', i.e. the process, and 'the writing', i.e. the product, to assess.

Again there is a need within your school for an agreed set of criteria to help teachers assess the development of early writers and writing. Here are some suggestions based on an amalgamation of the ideas from many schools and a text called *Dancing with the Pen*, which is produced by the Ministry of Education in New Zealand (1992) and is one of the most informative and user-friendly texts on writing available world wide. Note that we are using slightly different terminology here from the section on reading and describe the first stage as the 'emerging writer', for as soon as a mark is made the writer has begun. The second stage is then the 'developing writer'.

Attitude

The emerging writer

- Does the child enjoy playing at writing?
- Does the child show an awareness of the print in the classroom environment?
- Is the child using recognisable letters and numbers?
- Can you pinpoint the time when the child first used letter/sound knowledge?
- Is the child encouraged by his success and eager to write more?

The developing writer

- Does the child enjoy writing about a variety of topics?
- Does the child seek help and encouragement from others?
- Does the child show confidence in his ability to express himself in writing?
- Does the child expect people to enjoy reading his writing?
- Does the child find writing rewarding?

Understanding about print

The emerging writer

- Does the child understand about the orientation of a page?
- Does the child understand the purpose of spaces between words?
- Does the child know that print gives meaning?
- Does the child realise that stories can be written down?
- Does the child realise that writing can be read many times?

The developing writer

- Is the child beginning to understand the reasons for the use of capital letters, full-stops, question marks and commas?
- Is the child beginning to self-correct?
- Does the child understand that writing goes through a number of stages?
- Does the child realise that writing things down helps to clarify understanding?
- Does the child realise that writing follows a logical progression?

Ownership

The emerging and developing writer
- Does the child feel a sense of ownership for the writing?
- Does the child write freely about things that are important to him?
- Does the child try to search for ways to improve his writing?
- Does the child take writing home to share with his family?
- Does the child bring writing to school that has been done at home?

Ideas

The emerging writer
- Does the child draw pictures to generate ideas?
- Does the child talk about the pictures and ask you to write the text?
- Does the child attempt to write his ideas in simple sentences?

The developing writer
- Does the child talk about the topic in order to gather ideas?
- Does the child express himself in fluent sentences?
- Does the child have a concept of form, i.e. beginning, middle, end?

Modelling and assistance

The emerging writer
- Is the child learning to write by watching the teacher modelling writing?
- Does the child expect feedback from the teacher about his writing?

The developing writer
- Does the child use the modelled example as a starting point for his own text?
- Does the child expect feedback from his teacher and peers?
- Is the child prepared to re-work a piece of writing from time to time to produce something which gives great satisfaction?

When looking at *the writing* we need to address such criteria as:

- Does the writing say something?
- Does the writing have a purpose other than learning to write?
- Who was the audience for this piece of writing?
- Does the writing show a sequencing of ideas?
- Does the writing show evidence that the writer fits within one of the Gentry spelling stages?

How is this to be monitored?

As a staff you need to decide how you are going to organise all this and the coordinator needs to get things organised. Individuals will find their own user-friendly methods and this is fine as long as they suit the school policy. The involvement of the child in this is of great importance. Over years of observing young children learning, one becomes increasingly aware that little children do not see their own development as adults do. They see other children getting good at things, but few have awareness of their own development. If you, as coordinator, can sit down with a child and say for example, 'Just look how much more you can do now than before Christmas. Isn't this an interesting account of our assembly? Look how good you are getting at spelling, and haven't you been working hard at your handwriting?' This sort of conversation about writing can make all the difference to the child's self image. As coordinator you should be seen and heard to do this when you visit classrooms.

Throughout this book we have tried very hard not to be prescriptive, not to say do it this way or that, but a whole school approach will give the children the structure and stability they need as they pass from one class to the next. There can be nothing more confusing for a child than learning how to please one teacher and then passing onto another with a totally different regime and set of rules. How much better it is if there is a common pattern from class to class. Make sure that teachers have the same range of resources available in their classrooms. Children will enjoy writing on a variety of materials such as coloured paper cut into different shapes, squares, circles, triangles, raindrop shapes if writing about the rain, speech bubbles, lined paper, bordered letter paper, memos, sticky labels for messages. They love to make little books and staple them together with a hundred staples down the side . . . what most children like least, is the exercise book, especially the ones that have the school's name, logo and motto emblazoned on the front, because then the writing belongs to the school. Children love to write in colour, with felt pens, biros, coloured pencils. They particularly like to have brightly coloured special pencils that put magic into the writing. All classrooms need to have tools to tempt the children to write.

As coordinator you have to puzzle over how are all these papers of different shapes and sizes to be stored for each child. Remember the importance of consistency of approach. *A writing folder* for each child could be the answer. A folder with different sections in which to keep on-going work, finished work ready for publishing, work to go home. A folder in which to keep a small notebook, a 'Have a Go' book for try outs of spellings that the child is not sure of. A place to put a letter formation sheet showing where you start to write the letter for right and left handers. A phonic prompt sheet devised by the child with pictures of objects beginning with the letter sounds. Somewhere where the child can make a list of the words that they use often giving a visual reminder of spelling. A place to list the skills as they are acquired, e.g.

■ I can use full-stops in the right place.
■ I know how to use question marks.

In this way the child has all the things needed to make writing as successful as possible and they are all in one place. Gone are the days of a child wandering around looking for his 'writing' book, hunting for a pencil, searching for a spelling book, stopping for a chat and generally procrastinating. The teacher also has one place to look to refer to the child as a writer.

In one school the amount of money spent on books was cut drastically. Instead each child had a folder made of two sheets of card which lasted, with careful handling, for two years. The making of the folders was organised by a group of parents who incidentally found that stitching them together with dental floss prevented the card being torn! The proportions of the folders were carefully calculated so that two children could sit next to each other, each with their folder open. When they moved class, the folder, along with all the props went too. These were introduced into the reception class around Easter time, or when the teacher felt the children had developed the maturity to handle the idea. All writing was done in this way and topic work was then moved to a topic folder or pasted into a topic book.

It is vitally important that the children know why they are being asked to use a folder. A class of 6-year-olds, working in small groups and then reporting to the whole class, came up with this list of reasons why they should use their folders each time they did any writing.

- It will help us to keep our work together.
- You just get it out of the basket whenever you want to write.
- It's easy to find the sheets you want.
- You keep your finished and unfinished work in it.
- If your teacher is busy you just put your work in your folder.
- You can take good bits home to show your Mum.
- Your teacher can dip into it.
- It makes things easier.

The last reason sums everything up. It is possibly the most important reason of all. We should be making things easier for children in school. One would suggest that the writing folder use would not have been as successful as it was in that classroom if the teacher had not made the children think about what they were being asked to do. It also meant that the children were actively engaged in assessing their own work. They decided which pieces were good enough for publishing, they were in control.

So how is the evidence to be collected? Again, the National Literacy Framework advocates using guided writing sessions. Here are some suggestions in terms of the management of it.

- An exercise book to jot down observations of particular children for day to day use.

- These comments can then go into a file of each child's writing development.
- From the writing folder the child and teacher will select special examples to photocopy and keep as a record of progress. Not just the perfect finished product, but all the stages in the process of a special piece of work.
- Another excellent assessment guide is the child's 'Have a Go' book for spelling.

As coordinator you need to encourage teachers to talk about spelling. There comes a time in the child's spelling development when they know that a word doesn't look right. Suggest that they write the word themselves first, then search around the room and then ask the teacher. Most spelling books are arranged in alphabetical order to aid phonic awareness. If however they are just blank pages, perhaps one page per week with the date at the top, then the teacher and the child have a ready made assessment record of spelling development. The knowledgeable teacher just has to flick through the pages to see how the child attempts to spell unknown words. Also if a child has, for example spelt sun as 'sn' you can write the correct form and then encourage the child to think of other 'un' words and write them down together, thus extending the learning in context. This makes the 'Have a Go' book very user friendly.

Assessing children's writing is probably easier than making an accurate assessment of their speaking and listening abilities because at least you have the results to look at for as long as you need.

Children's achievements in speaking and listening

In this fast changing world, the essential skills of the future would seem to include the ability to think creatively, to express those ideas vocally and to be able to work collaboratively with others. Talk provides a most effective medium for learning. The links between talking and thinking cannot be emphasised strongly enough. Back in 1975, the Bullock Report 'A Language for Life', stressed the importance of using language to develop thinking skills.

❛ *A child is at a disadvantage in lacking the means to explain, describe, inquire, hypothesise, analyse, compare and deduce if language is seldom or never used for these purposes. This is the kind of language that is of particular importance to the forming of higher order concepts . . .*

Towards the end of Key Stage 1, children should be beginning to develop the skills to enable them to participate in collaborative group work. If this is an area that you have focused upon as a staff then everyone should be able to follow similar criteria and make notes whilst the children are actively engaged in group activities. For example, when working in small groups can the child:

- follow directions for getting into groups;
- use a quiet voice;
- listen attentively to what the other group members have to say;
- wait patiently for his turn to speak;
- articulate his thoughts clearly;
- stay on task;
- complete the task?

Whilst working individually, can the child;

- tell you clearly, exactly what he is doing;
- explain why he is doing it;
- tell you the steps he is taking to perform the task?

Whilst playing, can the child;

- share equipment;
- use language rather than force to get what he wants;
- explain and articulate a plan of action with his playmates;
- adapt his language, when engaged in role play, to fit the character he has become;
- play with language by making up rhymes and savouring words with an interesting sound?

1 If not, is there the possibility that the child might have a hearing impediment? Many children slip through the net.
2 If not, how are you, the coordinator, going to help the staff to structure activities in classrooms to help the children develop these vital skills?

3   If not, because many of the children have English as an additional language, what are you going to do to extend the children's knowledge in an enjoyable, motivating way?

Teacher observation has to be the best way to assess progress in this area and is really very easy to do whilst children are busy. This is another of the delights of whole class collaborative group work, for it gives teachers the opportunity to stand back, to listen and to observe.

Evaluating the data

Why is it that major assessment occurs mainly towards the end of the academic year when the results cannot benefit the way the children are being taught? Discovering that a child has a problem in May or June doesn't give much time to rectify the situation. This might seem simplistic but it has always been a puzzle. Surely the best time would be early in the year so that the results would provide information to help the individual child. Perhaps the thinking is that the next teacher will instantly see the need and plan appropriately, but in all honesty how many times do we hear colleagues say, 'Oh, I don't take much notice of the records, I like to make my own mind up about the children.' Perhaps November would be a good time to assess, once the children have settled into the new class and the teacher has become aware of individual differences. Or maybe just after Christmas because something strange happens to infants over the Christmas period, they seem to use the festive time to assimilate what they have learned and come back in January ready to apply that knowledge. It could be something to do with happiness, excitement and a stress free time providing a good environment for learning to be absorbed, but there again that could just be a fanciful thought. Certainly some kind of diagnostic assessment early in the school year would be advantageous.

In terms of assessing the curriculum provided by the school, evidence collected through the SAT can be analysed in terms of any areas of English in which a significant number of children may show strength or weakness. This can lead to improvements in the curriculum for the following year.

Moderation

Teachers have always, in one way or another, assessed their pupils' work. What we need to develop is a way to standardise that assessment within the school so that high flyers, steady workers and strugglers can be recognised and encouraged.

Perhaps before we even get into a discussion on moderation we need to talk about *expectations*. As a coordinator for English, you need to be sure that everyone who comes into contact with the children has very high expectations of the children as users of English. Children can achieve their potential if teachers expect them to. What often comes into play to mar this is teacher stress. If teachers are up tight because the school did not achieve a good national rating, then that stress level will be reflected in the children. Young children especially, have an uncanny ability to absorb the atmosphere of their surroundings. If you are happy and relaxed then the children probably have a good day too. If you are tearing your hair out about 'falling standards' then the children will probably be unsettled and distracted. You only have to observe the effect of a windy day to see the reality of this, they come rushing into the classroom like a whirlwind. Windy days are lively days. Humans respond to a stimulus and if we don't expect much, then that is what we will get.

Therefore, make sure that the teachers set high expectations. Plan for success, encourage the pessimistic, prod the complacent, develop a feeling of optimism within the school. Yes, these children can achieve, by a wide variety of motivational means. Extend your influence beyond the teaching staff to make sure that in your school it is made perfectly clear that reading and writing are never used as a form of punishment. Just explain to the ancillary staff why this has such negative connotations and they will understand. You'll probably find the school miscreants all doing maths until the maths coordinator realises what's going on. Literacy experiences in your school must be positive experiences.

This is where we can learn from a study of comparative education. In the East there is a Confucian belief that through hard work one can achieve, that failure is not a reflection of your intellectual ability but rather is put down to the fact that you just didn't work hard enough. Yes, there are casualties along the way, but most children have a very high self esteem as learners and a sense of responsibility right from the day they start school. A lot has been said about the success of Eastern students. Brief visits have been made to schools in Taiwan and Japan and the ability of the children has been attributed to the instructional way they are taught. It is more likely that the value the culture puts on education and the support of the families causes the results. People have high expectations which lead to achievement. This is the rationale behind the Literacy Strategy, to address the 'long tail' of under-achievement by giving all children the opportunity to succeed.

Accepting that your teachers are all well motivated and thinking positively, how is the coordinator to moderate their evaluation of the achievement of the children across year bands?

What you need to do is to get groups of teachers to look at specific examples of pupils' work and compare and discuss until common criteria can be arrived at. Moderating in this way leads to consistency within the school which will benefit the children. If teachers have similar expectations it then assists the child's progression from one teacher to the next.

Let's look at the steps a coordinator needs to follow when planning a moderation meeting.

1 Ask teachers to bring a cross-section of work from the very able, average and lower achievement levels.
2 As a group, look at the pupils' work including any teacher notes which tell you the situation in which it was done.
3 Together, look carefully at the criteria for assessment.
4 The information on SAT's current criteria are necessary for interpreting the statements of attainment. Make sure everybody understands what is meant in terms of specific objectives and criteria for assessment.
5 Discuss the possible levels, encouraging teachers to use and become familiar with the terminology involved.

6 Agree the level that the group feels is appropriate for each piece of work.

7 Then take a random sample of work and agree on the level.

As with all meetings, have a fixed time limit and stick to it. Regular moderation meetings will then not be seen as a burden but a helpful experience and will become positive time. In any situation where work is being assessed a moderation component is essential. After a while it becomes an accepted part of the assessment procedure. It is a good idea for the coordinator to develop a portfolio of moderated work for teacher reference, this enables colleagues to make comparisons, gain confidence and leaves you free from constant referrals.

The use of portfolios

In all the discussions so far on how we are to monitor children's achievement, the underlying two questions are:

1 Why are we doing it?

2 How can we help the children?

Portfolios are one way to reflect the growing achievements of the learner, *but* beware that the portfolio does not start to dominate the curriculum, if it does then it is no better than a test. What often happens is that teachers start to teach to the needs of the portfolio, which should *reflect* the teaching, not drive it. It is also important that the evidence stored should be a true picture of the child's work not just a perfect final copy. The drafts that went before should be there.

As with everything, portfolios work if they are given high status. They should be a resource belonging to the child, the contents of which are negotiated with the teacher. Obviously with very young children they have more of a resemblance to a teacher's file, but the child can still have a say in what is stored and rejected.

What should go into the portfolio?

Writing, writing and more writing! If we accept that writing, even at the beginning stage, is an expression of thought, then what a wonderful record of the developing person we have in this early writing. Obviously significant work should be kept, but at least one piece per month, clearly dated, would give an overview of development. Apart from the secretarial skills of handwriting and spelling, try to find pieces that capture the essence of the child. Pieces that display the child using writing for different purposes and different audiences. Include writing that is significant and where necessary jot down information about the situation in which it was written. Anything that clearly relates to the SAT criteria would obviously be of use. Each time a piece of writing is added just look back and see how the child is developing and make a note with reference to the observational criteria mentioned earlier. Tell the children why you are doing this, include them in the selection and confer with the child about their writing at the same time. If writing folders are in use in the classrooms then this makes the selection process very easy because the children are writing on sheets of paper which can easily be transferred. As each spelling 'Have a Go' book is completed then they too can be added to the portfolio as a record of progress in spelling.

Reading can be represented by the 'running record' or other method of regular appraisal in use. It would also be a good idea to keep an audio tape for each child and record them involved in a shared reading from time to time. Just an idea, but admittedly at bit time consuming. A short list of books that have been significant in the child's development as a reader would also be of use along with any form of completed dialogue book that goes backwards and forwards between home and school.

This is another point in the book where one can almost hear the reader screaming, 'Where am I supposed to keep 36 portfolios?' A good point. Where indeed. This is where such innovations require very careful strategic planning on the part of the coordinator well in advance of the introduction of the scheme. Portfolios have to be stored somewhere that:
- has easy access for children and teacher;
- is strong enough to hold quite a weight and protect the portfolios from damage;
- doesn't take up too much room.

Suggestion

Portfolios
One final word on the subject of portfolios and that is keep one for yourself. Save significant pieces of work that children have done as a result of your teaching or policies. You never know when they will come in useful for assignments, if engaged in further study, or examples for a book.

The most obvious solution would be to have a filing cabinet in each classroom specifically for assessment. The bottom two or three drawers could then be used for the portfolios with each child having a hanging file. Great care would need to be taken when opening and shutting the drawers to ensure that children didn't get their fingers trapped and that only one drawer was opened at once, but experience has shown that they soon get used to the system.

If this is a new idea to your colleagues then the coordinator would need to persuade a colleague to trial the system for a term in order to tell other members of staff about it. It would also give one teacher the opportunity to deal with initial problems and to streamline the system for the needs of the school, before everyone is asked to do it. Your role as coordinator would be to monitor and lend support. Remember, it is a good idea to use other colleagues to 'sell ideas' to the staff — there's much more chance of a smooth acceptance if you are not continuously telling them of the wonders of your latest great idea.

At the end of the year it would have to be decided just how much went up to the next class. Portfolios could resemble suitcases by the time the children reached primary six if you are not careful. A whole school policy decision would be needed here.

Storing the data

One way of dealing with the volume of data on each child would be to make use of modern technology and put everything onto a networked computer system within the school. Teachers could login with a password and have access to all the information they need without having to leave the classroom and carry heavy files around. There would be far more likelihood that colleagues would actually access the information if it was accessible at the touch of a keyboard button. One could then take things a step further and imagine a child's portfolio being scanned at the end of every year and kept on disc. The child could then take home the hard copy to keep. Think of the paper and space that would be saved.

Reporting to parents

Before beginning to address the face-to-face discussion of a child's progress with the parents there is a lot that needs to be said about parental involvement in the learning progress of their children. Traditionally, the role the parent can play in this evaluation procedure has been ignored. If we want to redress the balance then we have to make sure that parents are fully informed about not only *what* their children are learning, but *how* it will take place.

At Key Stage 1 you have an advantage because parents are usually interested and eager to be involved when their children begin school. If possible, this should start as early as possible during the year *before* the children begin. Invite the parents to the school and talk to them about the things they can be doing at home to pave the way for a smooth transition into formal learning. There are many areas to cover, but the specifics for English could be decided upon quite quickly over a cup of coffee with the reception class teachers. It goes without saying that the priorities will differ from school to school, but there is no harm in stating the ideal situation, after all we need to have high expectations. Here are some suggestions gleaned from discussions with coordinators that could be put together into a non-threatening, helpful booklet.

Reporting to parents

- Give the parents a copy of the correct letter formation for the handwriting style favoured by your school. Impress upon them the importance of the correct form when the child learns to write her or his own name. Explain fully why this is so important. Tell them to help the child to recognise this pattern of letters that give the child their own identity.
- Talk about ways to make the child to become aware of print in the environment. For example tell the parents to explain how it is you know which bus to catch, how the postman knows which house to deliver letters to, how reading the paper helps you find the time of a favourite TV programme etc. These examples need to be specifically related to the child's experiences so that he can see that learning to read will be an advantageous thing to do.
- Suggest that instead of being a nuisance in the supermarket, the pre-school child can be encouraged to help the adult to hunt for a few, easily recognised, favourite food items and when found say, 'Yes, baked beans, well done, look it says it on the can to help us'. Things like this need to be seen as a game which also relieve the boredom of the young child and make life a lot easier for the parent.
- Encourage the parents to tell their children stories. They don't have to be traditional stories, often family incidents beginning 'when I was a little girl' will captivate the child. This encourages the enjoyment of storytelling which is such an important early stage in the reading process.

- Talk about sharing books, about being aware that parents are a role model. If they see their parents gaining pleasure from a book then children are more likely to discover that pleasure themselves.
- Encourage them to take their children to the public library, to let them browse and select for themselves, to take home a favourite book over and over again. Talk to the parents about children for whom such experiences have been stimulating. Real examples carry weight. One that comes to mind is of a boy who, from the age of eighteen months, used to borrow books from the travelling library. He and his mother used to watch in the window every other Thursday for the mobile library to go up the road to turn around and then rush out to wait for it to stop outside their group of houses. For the three years before that little boy attended school he was a regular 'reader'. Books were an important part of his daily life and when he went to school he became a 'real' reader as naturally as he had acquired speech. It has to be said that, at the time, the neighbours thought his mother was a little odd, but you need to be thick skinned sometimes for the good of your children.
- Talk about the specifics of bookish behaviour, of holding the book the right way up, of starting at the beginning not the end. This can be a serious matter when children are used to seeing adults flicking through magazines from the back to the front, of left to right orientation, of pictures giving clues to meaning.

Make the sessions welcoming, friendly, informative and not too long. There is only so much that one can absorb and important messages need to hit the mark.

Once the children have started school the coordinator needs to invite the parents in and talk to them in a straightforward, informative way to tell them exactly how you go about literacy learning with their children and the reasons why you adopt this approach, so that they can be encouraged to use the same methods when they are helping their children at home. Emphasise the great importance the home plays, that it is a partnership forged for the good of the children. Be careful not to make the parents feel inadequate because, when you think about it, all the theorising is based on good common sense that observant parents take for granted.

Do these sessions regularly once a term. Start with a general talk in September or October about literacy development and then hit issues that are specific to the needs of the children, the parents and the school in the second and third terms. Perhaps do one on the development of writing, with lots of examples of writing done by the children in your school, where parents are encouraged to celebrate and praise the early efforts rather than being negative and focusing on errors. On another occasion take an hour to talk the parents through the Gentry spelling stages, again with light hearted examples of writing their own children have done. When the parents are informed about the process, the formal reporting of achievement is more understandable and will therefore have a beneficial effect upon the child.

If such a system of informal curriculum sessions is not a feature in your school, then getting this started should be a priority for the coordinator. Finding the right time to do this is an issue. If you feel that it is something really important, then a time has to be found that suits the parents. If both parents work during the day, then an early evening slot might be the best. If you think that it is important that both parents get the message, then you might have to do a repeat 'performance' on a second night so that both parents get the chance to attend, albeit separately. One useful tip on running such sessions. If they are at the end of a school day when you are not exactly fresh, the adrenalin carries you through the presentation but seems to disappear as soon as you stop speaking. If you then take questions from the floor and get involved in a contentious issue, it is possible to undo all the good you have done by being unprepared. Far better to allow half hour for informal questioning with members of staff involved to break the group up into smaller, informal groups. Don't let this drag on, stop the meeting at the appointed time. Parents and staff will be more willing to attend if you start and end on time.

When it comes to report writing and face to face interviews it is important to stress to colleagues the need to be specific about the learning stage the child has reached, with reference to examples from the child's portfolio. Do be careful though, when discussing such young children, that you take maturity levels into account. Some small children seem to have a built in safety device that stops them doing things they are not ready to attempt. Parents can very quickly be panicked into thinking their child has a problem when all that is really needed is more time. This is why very careful monitoring of the child's literacy progress by observation and agreed procedures is so important. Before a teacher voices concern to parents it is better that you are involved to review the child's progress. What happens so often is that parents find it impossible to hide their concern from the child who then suffers a loss of self esteem. If there is a real problem then you can be sure that the parents will have picked it up first and they will probably raise the issue first. Do emphasise to staff that they should, for this reason, pay particular attention to the concerns parents raise.

Many schools draw up a contract between parents and school for joint responsibility in sharing reading time with children. This then leads to the opportunity for parents to become actively involved in assessing and evaluating the progress of their own child.

Reporting to the junior department

In a mixed infant/junior school there should be few problems in the transition from Key Stage 1 to 2. It is assumed that there would be a consistent school policy towards literacy development, so the move should be a smooth one for the children. There are however, situations where the infant school is a totally separate entity and links will have to be forged to ensure that your knowledge about the children is shared with the new school.

Successful schools

In schools that succeed, the features described are in place. On a classroom level, successful classrooms flourish where the teacher is a skilful classroom manager. With all the added demands on today's teachers, emphasis has to be placed on good forward planning, the efficient use of time so that children are on task for as long as possible, a combination of individual, small group and class teaching to fit the objectives of what is to be taught and established routines that work for the benefit of the children. The school year needs to be viewed and points of stress highlighted so that staff don't flounder from one crisis point to the next. Above all, in successful situations, assessment is a continuous process, which leads to evaluation being made, which leads to a fine tuning of practice, which gives us happy successful learners.

Part five | Resources for learning

Chapter 11
Managing resources and facilities

Managing resources and facilities

Resourcing is such a vital aspect of good teaching that it is important to spend time considering issues. Some of the issues are so 'obvious' that to discuss them at length can be unnecessary. Then again, in some schools teachers talk of little in their teaching beyond resources, spend ages organising them, moan about not having enough, and always want more. Thinking about resources can be done strategically, rather than from a problem point of view.

Resources for children

What you need to do first of all is to do an inventory of current resources. You need to know what you have already got before a plan is made for additional expenditure. Perhaps over a holiday time you could call for all English resources to be taken to the school hall in order that they can be recorded. You will be amazed at what comes out of the woodwork. People are naturally acquisitive — like magpies — and the strangest things will turn up. This will help you to discover resources in existence that might be unused or underused. If they are unused because they are in a very poor condition or belong to the last century, then throw them out. Be ruthless. The last thing you want is valuable space being taken up with piles of redundant material. There might be a need for some of this material elsewhere in the world. Some schools recycle reading scheme books to countries who put out world-wide appeals for second-hand reading material in English.

When recording what you have got in stock you need to look at such criteria as:

- publication date;
- quantity;
- suitable age group;
- where is it being used at the moment;
- how often;
- physical state.

Be wary of publication dates, look at the first date of publication and decide whether the material is still relevant. The quantity and physical condition of essential items is critical in establishing a system of regular renewal. It could be that, for example, multiple copies of sets of books were ordered all at the same time. Rather than being faced in five years' time with the crisis of replacements being needed all at once, it might be an idea to restock regularly. This is particularly important with expensive items like 'Big Books'.

You might find that in the days before you took up appointment, teachers ordered for 'personal need'. Staff at Key Stage 1 frequently move between classes and there could well be someone who ordered equipment for use with Year 2 but is now teaching reception and has a cupboard full of little-used material. Such a census should flush out these hoards. You will need the firm backing of the headteacher when you do this because it is an area that could be fraught with conflict. It needs to be made quite clear that these resources are the property of the school, not the individual teacher. On the other hand the coordinator has to see the point that it is frustrating to have given time and thought to ordering and then lose the lot to someone who didn't bother.

What you really need to be thinking of is a move towards central resourcing so that teachers have a core of essential equipment, and then access to that which they need on a limited time frame. This will far better match the needs of the children to their level of achievement. What sort of equipment should each teacher have in the classroom?

- Lots and lots of books!
- alphabet friezes;
- a set of photocopiable handwriting worksheets of the agreed style;
- a variety of picture dictionaries;
- a strong, serviceable tape recorder and headsets so that children can listen to tapes;
- a strong easel approximately 1 metre high for Big Book sharing and modelling writing, (Some would say that a white board serves the purpose, but you can't staple the writing together for future reference if it is wiped clean every half hour or so);
- pencils, felt pens, crayons and vast quantities of paper of different colours and thickness;
- a carpet and cushions for the book corner;
- wall mounted book display racks;
- containers for storing equipment, writing folders, portfolios etc.;
- a comfortable chair to share a book with a child;
- computers and software;
- a copy of the National Curriculum for English;
- a copy of the school policy document for English.

In the central store you would put such items as:
- puzzles and games. There will have to be some sort of arrangement that they will be used in different year bands so that the children have access to fresh stimuli;
- language games that encourage visual awareness and speaking and listening skills;
- cassettes of stories, poems etc. with their accompanying text;
- videos;
- reading scheme books, or would you store those in the library because a book is a book is a book . . . ?;
- Big Books and the sets of their smaller equivalent texts.

Something you will unfortunately have to think about is security. It could be that the only available space is a big cupboard, so would all staff have a key? Would they sign materials in and out? Things to discuss with colleagues. Of course, if you had the luxury of a whole room, then it could become an English learning centre. Whole new vistas open up.

Then there is the issue of how the resources you have match with the school policy. You have to approach the subject of needs. What do we need to put this policy into effect? Well, one thing that will be the same in all schools is the need for lots of books. What sort of books?

The National Literacy Framework emphasises the need for a range of reading in each term. In Year 2, term 3, children should be working with extended stories by significant children's authors, different stories by the same author, text with language play, such as riddles, tongue-twisters, humorous verse and stories. This list, term by term, of range in reading gives an ideal checklist against which you can measure the quality of the book stock.

Will you be using a published scheme as a backbone and lots of picture books, in which case you need careful criteria for their selection and multiple copies of books that work well. One of the reasons why the 'Real Book' debate became so controversial arose because some schools switched approach before they had adequate numbers of good texts. Schools that use the approach successfully have large reserves of books so that they have, in effect, developed their own structured 'scheme' using books that children really like to read. This is a prime example of how a new initiative has to be planned over a period of time and must not be rushed into, resourced by enthusiasm alone.

Once you have done a stock take and re-distributed useful items, sit down with staff and talk about items you and they feel are needed, with reference to the National Literacy Framework, well before the deadline for requisitions. Develop a systematic approach to spending based on projected needs not on crisis due to shortages.

Be very, very careful about buying sets of books where you only get a couple of inspection copies for a series. Publishers will often send out the best volumes and others might not be so good. Check the quality of the paper, print size, level of language used, illustrations and binding before buying books.

Offer your help to colleagues in other curriculum areas who are buying texts. Make sure that the language of instruction will be understandable for the children in your school. Mathematics books particularly need careful vetting. To a second language infant a question like, 'How many sparrows are there?' might elicit a blank look, but 'How many birds are there?' will be perfectly understandable. There is no suggestion that children should only have sparse texts, but in some subject areas the quality of the language used is vital for understanding. What is often put to the test is not mathematical knowledge, but knowledge about language.

When buying books that will be used on a daily basis cover them with tacky back to prolong their life. This can double the time they can be used and is money well spent. You do need someone with the expertise and time to do all the covering for you. Applying the plastic cover is easy when you know how, but is the subject of a sticky tragedy if entrusted to someone who doesn't know how to apply the stuff, wrinkle free. It is very expensive, but will save money in replacement texts.

The number of computers you have in each classroom will probably be beyond your control. They are an incredibly motivating resource to get children writing. Those who have problems with fine motor control are often terrific at using a keyboard to express themselves. Children love to see their efforts printed. It is a great incentive for writing and a valuable resource for developing reading skills too. Put a small group of children together to write a story using the computer and you can hear them sharing knowledge about spelling and grammar as well as sharing the structure of the story. In terms of reading, interactive 'talking books' are a great attraction (as long as we can focus children on the print as well as letting them play with the pictures). In addition there is software available which enables you to produce your own 'talking books' with children in guided writing sessions. Such texts can be sequels to well known stories ('The Hungry Giant 2 . . . The Return') or based on patterned texts read and explored in the Literacy Hour.

We have touched on the issue of libraries a number of times. If your school has a library that's great, but who does the book ordering, and where does the budget come from? The English coordinator should really be selecting the books. Become a regular subscriber to magazines about new publications in the area of children's literature. Keep an eye on the professional publications as well. Try to visit your local bookshop and generally browse through the books. Some bookshops are happy to give a discount if you buy direct and spend a largish sum of money. Shop around and seek out good deals. Try to avoid buying unknown texts from catalogues, it's better to get your hands and eyes on the books themselves. If you find a new book that fits your criteria for Key Stage 1 readers, then buy three or four copies, you need to build up stocks of books that work. Remember, you are looking for interesting texts where the words and the pictures work together to give meaning. Books that have natural repetition and rhythm, have meaningful, natural language and above all have child appeal. For example, the Literacy Framework expects children in Year 1, term 2, to meet traditional stories and rhymes, fairy stories, stories and poems with predictable, patterned language, including playground chants, verse from other cultures, and plays. Also, look carefully for non-fiction texts that meet these requirements. Children don't have to grow on a diet of stories, variety in the menu is the best approach. The range of reading needs to include all manner of texts from recipes, to charts, to diaries, to instructions on how to make models, to atlases, to lists of books in the catalogues.

Funding

Go for it and get as much as you can. Let's face it, literacy is the key issue in early education so ask for as much as you need and a little more. Your choice of materials to buy must be made based on clearly stated criteria. Beware of travelling representatives of publishing houses. If you want to let them into your school then tell them the type of material you are looking for before they come. Also, make sure you have the final word on what is ordered, otherwise staff will flick through inspection copies and not look closely enough. What you buy must reflect your needs. There is not so much danger of this at Key Stage 1 because hopefully, you are using less textbook material in English.

Keep your eyes open for sources of external funding. If your PTA raises lots of money, then ask for a regular donation for the library. Involve the children in fund-raising activities for the benefit of the school. Take every opportunity going to fill your school with books that the children have easy access to.

Resources for teachers

To ensure teacher confidence in the area of English you need to build up a resource of books, articles, videos etc. Home produced videos would be great. Use the skill of the teachers you've got and video them in action. These are far more useful than mass produced material that only addresses some of your needs. They also give an accurate introduction for new staff or long-term supply teachers.

As has been said earlier, you must build up a reference library for staff. Keep your eyes on reviews and buy books to cover the English curriculum; make sure you don't just stock up on books about reading. Keep a track of who has got what and for how long they have had the book. We are good at nagging children to return books but not so good as a profession at doing it ourselves.

One way of getting teachers to really enjoy their teaching in English is to get them to read about it. To talk about what they have read is a real point of breakthrough. To encourage reading, staff debate, and developing practice, one area to consider is to ask different teachers to read short, interesting articles on related aspects of English teaching say, using imaginative play, to instigate discussion. A short piece each, nothing too daunting, well chosen texts . . . sounds like good teaching!

A final word, or two

Being English coordinator, especially at Key Stage 1, puts you at the very hub of the young child's learning. It is a really rewarding job that will keep you very busy. Find every opportunity you can to get out and about meeting other coordinators. Share ideas, get concerns off your chest, attend local conferences and insist that from time to time you are allowed to attend the big UK based international conferences on literacy that are organised by UKRA and NATE. There is a real need for more practising teachers to attend such conferences to talk to publishers and researchers about the real needs in primary schools.

When you've been in the job for a while, and you have achieved those things you set out to do, then look around and move on, don't stay too long, go out on a high and spread the word somewhere else. As a teacher you are a valuable resource for children everywhere.

References

AIKEN, J. (1975) *A Necklace of Raindrops*, London: Puffin.

BRYANT, P. and BRADLEY, L. (1985) *Children's Reading Problems*, Oxford: Basil Blackwell.

BENNETT, A. (1994) *Writing Home*, London: Faber.

BULLOCK REPORT (1975) London: HMSO.

CAMBOURNE, B. (1988) *The Whole Story*, Ashton: Scholastic.

CAMBOURNE AND TURBILL (1997) Paper presented at the UKRA Conference, Newcastle, UK.

CLARK, M. (1976) *Young Fluent Readers*, London: Heinemann Educational.

CRIPPS AND COX (1989) *Joining the ABC*, LDA.

DONALDSON, M. (1978) *Children's Minds*, London: Collins/Fontana.

FOX, C. (1993) At the Very Edge of the Forest, The Influence of *Literature on Storytelling by Children*, London: Cassell.

FRITH, U. (1980) *Cognitive Processes in Spelling*, London: Academic Press.

FULLAN, M. (1991) *The New Meaning of Educational Change*, London: Cassell Educational Limited.

GENTRY, R. (1987) *Spel is a 4 letter Word*, Oxford: Heinemann.

GOSWAMI, U. and BRYANT, P. (1990) *Phonological Skills and Learning to Read*, Hillsdale, NJ: Erlbaum and Associates.

HARDY, B. (1977) Essay: 'Narrative as a primary act of mind' in *The Cool Web*, Meek, B., Warlow, A., Barton, G. (eds), London: Bodley Head.

HARRISON, C. and COLES, M. (1992) *The Reading for Real Handbook*, London: Routledge.

JAGER ADAMS, M. (1990) *Beginning to Read*, Cambridge, Mass: MIT.

LITERACY FRAMEWORK (1998) London: HMSO.

MEEK, M. (1991) *On Being Literate*, London: The Bodley Head.

MEEK, M. and MILLS, C. (1988) *Language and Literacy in the Primary School*, Lewes: Falmer Press.

MOORE, I. (1990) *Six Dinner Sid*, London: Simon and Schuster.

MINISTRY OF EDUCATION (NEW ZEALAND) (1992) *Dancing with the Pen, the Learner as a Writer*, Wellington: Learning Media.

READ, C. (1986) *Children's Creative Spelling*, London: Routledge and Kegan Paul.

SENDAK, M. (1970) *Where The Wild Things Are*, London: Penguin Books.

TORRINGTON AND HALL (1987) *Personnel Management: A New Approach*, London: Prentice-Hall.

VYGOTSKY, L. S. (1962) *Thought and Language*, Cambridge, MA: Massachusetts Institute of Technology.

WATERLAND, L. (1985) *Read with Me: An Apprenticeship Approach to Reading*, Stroud: Thimble Press.

WILSON, D. (1992) *A Strategy of Change: Concepts and Controversies in the Management of Change*, London: Routledge.

WOODWARD, H. (1993) *Negotiated Evaluation*, Oxford: Heinemann.

Big Books

Buster McCluster, Badger Publishing.

Goldilocks and the Three Bears, Kingscourt Publishers.

The Hungry Giant, Story Chest.

Nursery Rhymes

Ross, T. Oscar Got The Blame, Arrow.

Cowley, J. Mrs Wishy Washy, Story Chest.

Cowley, J. The King's Pudding.

Williams, S. I Went Walking, Red Wagon.

Eggleton, J. Rat-a-Tat-Tat.

Index

achievement 160–83
activities
  book displays 14–15
  environmental print 21
  name displays 15
  playscripts 147
  poetry 148–9
  policy document guidelines
    113
  Teddy Bears' Picnic 22–3
  writing 20
agendas 62
Ahlberg, A. 86
Ahlberg, J. 86
alliteration 164
alphabet friezes 81, 189
ancillary staff 175
anecdotal notes 162
announcements 19
appointment of coordinators 8,
  10
assessment 121, 141–50
  baseline 151–9
  standards 174–5
assistants 131, 137, 146
attainment 1, 155–9, 176
  see also achievement
attitude 167
audio tapes 178

auditory perception 120
audits 12–14, 16, 110
Australia 16, 76
availability timetables 49

background of schools 111–12
baseline assessment 151–9
bedtime stories 73–4
beginning readers 163–4
beliefs 69–93
Bennett, A. 74
Big Books 16–19, 90–2, 113
  budgets 56
  emerging readers 164
  modelling lessons 24–48
  restocking 188, 189
  storage 122
biscuits 62
Blake, Q. 81
bookmarks 86, 114
books 80–1, 85, 112
  achievement 160
  buying 55
  care of 118
  choosing 163–4
  displays 14–15, 81, 120
  reading corners 117–18
  resources 189–91
  role models 180

treatment 181
  see also text selection
bookshops 192
boys 120, 154, 157
Bradley, L. 84
*Brown Bear, Brown Bear What Do
    You See?* 93
Brown, R. 86, 93
Browne, A. 86
Bryant, P. 83, 84
budgets 55–6, 92, 192
Bullock Report 70–1, 171–3
Burningham, J. 86
Buster McCluster 53–4
buying books 190–3
  see also text selection

cakes 62, 125
Cambourne, B. 18, 115, 142, 162
Campbell, R. 86
Canada 76
captions 96
care of books 118
caretakers 9–10
Carle, E. 86
carpets 117, 189
case studies
  Big Books 17–19, 24–48
  explicit learning 51–4
catalogues 192
charts 19
child-centred learning 83–93
children 9
  assessment 141–3, 146–50
  books 189
  confidence 127
  curriculum 50–4
  displays 14–15
  English as an additional
    language 101–2
  entitlement 119–20
  environment 80–1
  folders 170–2
  foundations 77–9
  home 72–3

  learning experiences 83–93
  modelling writing 16, 21–3
  planning 12
  portfolios 177–9, 182
  reading 17–19
  reading ages 160
  reports 179–83
  resources 187–92
  self-image 169
  special needs 103–4
  writing achievement 166–72
choosing books 163–4
  see also text selection
Clarke, M. 72
classroom organisation 117–18
Clay, M. 162
cleaning staff 9–10
Cloze analysis 162
coat pegs 14
Cole, B. 86
collaboration *see* group work
colleagues
  data evaluation 174
  environmental print 82–3
  foundations 79
  influencing 123
  INSET 58
  Literacy Framework 96
  modelling writing 21–3
  planning 12, 49
  policy documents 109, 111
  portfolios 179
  resources 190
  socialising 9
  staff development 71
colouring 116
communication skills 64–5
comparative education 175–6
complacency 123, 175
composition 129, 130
comprehension 129, 130, 156
computers 20, 93, 179, 189, 191
concentration 77
concept maps 146, 147
conferences 194

confidence 1, 9, 24, 61
  beliefs 72, 79, 86
  book selection 81
  observation 163
  planning 127, 131
  special needs 104
  spelling 124
  writing 87, 167
conflict 63–4, 113–14, 188
Confucianism 176
consistency 63, 79, 110
  achievement 176
  junior departments 183
  policy documents 114, 120–1
  writing 166
contracts 183
cookery books 20
coordinator role 1–2, 5–7, 8–10
core purpose 7
course leaders 57–9
courses 50, 112, 124–5
Cowley, J. 17, 47
Cox 87, 88
Cripps 87, 88
criterion referenced tests 161
curriculum
  coverage 2, 131
  evenings 16, 121
  initiative 50–6
  Key Stage 1 1
  segmentation 97
  sessions 57–62, 182
Curriculum Development Plans 58
cushions 117, 189

Dancing with the Pen 166
The Dark, Dark Wood 93
data evaluation 174–6
deadlines 116
decision-making 142
developing writers 167, 168
development planning 134–7
dialogue books 86, 178
diaries 120–1
displays 14–15

Donaldson, M. 73, 84
drama 135

easels 16–19, 63
  child-centred learning 82
  policy documents 113
  resources 189
educational press 92
effectiveness 141
Eggleton, J. 89
elephant story 102
emerging readers 164
emerging writers 20, 167, 168
engagement 18
English as an additional language
    101–2, 119, 154, 174
enlarged texts 16
entitlement 119–20
entrance lobbies 14
envelopes 20
environmental print 21, 73, 77,
    80–3
equipment 60, 122, 173, 188–9
evaluation 121, 141, 142
evidence of achievement 160–83
expectations 6, 6–7, 175, 176
explicit learning 50–6, 76, 83
  assessment 143, 150
  folders 171
  portfolios 178
eye contact 61

facilities 187–95
families 72, 176
favourite books 81, 163, 164
feedback 16, 49, 168
fiction 129, 130
flash cards 84, 161
folders 170–2
follow-up sessions 57
foundations of learning 72–9
Fox, C. 85
Frith, U. 84
full-stops 167, 170
Fullan, M. 12

funding 57, 58, 124, 192–3
furniture 59, 61, 189

gender 120
Gentry, R. 88
Gentry spelling stages 169, 181
gifted children 75–6, 103, 119–20, 162
girls 120, 154, 157
goals 11
Goldilocks and the Three Bears 42–7
good practice 14, 71, 123
Goodman 162
Goswami, U. 83, 84
governors 109
grammar 17, 94, 129–30, 191
graphemes 84
Graves, D. 115
group work 24, 77–9, 82, 173–4
guided reading 165
guided writing 171
guidelines for policy documents 112–15

Hall 11
halls 59, 187
handouts 49
Hardy, B. 102
Harrison, C. 85
Have a Go books 170, 172, 178
headteachers 8–11
  conflict 63, 114
  INSET 58
  Literacy Framework 104
  planning 16
  policy documents 109, 111
  resources 188
  statistical analysis 152
hearing impediments 173
history 97–100, 125
home 72–7, 81, 86
  dialogue books 178
  folders 171
  learning progress 180

links 120–1
  policy documents 114–15
  reading 164
  target setting 158–9
  writing 168
home corner 90
home–school contracts 183
The Hungry Giant 35–7, 113, 191
Hutchins, P. 86

I Went Walking 90, 91, 92, 93
ideas 168
identification of special needs 103–4
illustrators 86
implementation 12
in-house appointments 10
in-service training (INSET) 57–62, 112, 124
incrementalism 11
independent reading 113
indicators 162
individual work 173
information technology (IT) 121
innovation 64, 110, 178
inspections 2
instructions 96
interpersonal skills 63
inventories 187

Japan 176
job descriptions 10–13, 122
journals 92, 192
junior departments 183

key outcomes 7
Key Stage 2 11, 101, 183
key statements 72–93, 94
The King's Pudding 47–8

labels 19, 80, 96
leadership 6, 7, 57–9
learning
  centres 190
  environments 111

needs 70–1, 87–8, 101–2, 119–20
objectives 146
outcomes 150
LEAs 109, 151–2, 154–5
left-handed children 119
lesson planning 24, 133–4
letter formation 15, 87, 170, 180
level descriptors 1
libraries 55, 81, 92, 117
  achievement 180–1
  recommended reading 122
  resources 189, 191–2, 193
life expectancy of displays 15
Lindblom 11
listening 77, 79, 97
  achievement 172–4
  planning 134, 135, 137
  policy documents 113
lists 19, 96, 118
literacy
  acquisition 6
  assessment 142
  beliefs 69–93
  classroom organisation 117–18
  coordinators 1–2
  experiences 19–23
  foundations 72
  lesson planning 134
  methods 75–6
  skills 125
  success 115–16
  teacher training 7
  time allocation 118–19
Literacy Framework 2, 69, 94–104
  achievement 165
  beliefs 71, 85
  planning 128, 135
  policy documents 112–14
  resources 190, 192
  success 116
  writing 171
Literacy Hour 2, 24, 95
  assessment 144, 145–50
  beliefs 83

  planning 128
  policy documents 113
  resources 191–2
Literacy Strategy 2, 12, 69
  achievement 176
  planning 128–30
long-term planning 128, 135, 137
lost readers 162
Lower School Units 11

McKee, D. 86
McRae, R. 89
magazines 19, 92, 192
management
  meetings 62–5
  resources 187–95
  teams 9
marking 146
Martin, B. 93
mathematics 118–19, 125, 175, 191
maturity levels 182
meaning 72
medium-term planning 128–30
Meek, M. 74
meetings 62–5
methods 70–1, 73–4
  child-centred learning 89–92
  English as an additional language 101
  environmental print 81–2
  foundations 78–9
Ministry of Education, New Zealand 166
miscue analysis 162
mobility of pupils 158
modelling 16, 18–19, 21–4
  displays 48–9
  lessons 24–48, 63, 103
  writing 82, 113, 122, 168
moderation 175–7
monitoring 121, 141, 142, 169–72, 181
Moore, I. 96

mother tongue speakers 101–2
motivation 6, 175
Mrs Wishy Washy 37–41, 122
Muslims 102

names 15, 180
narrative 102, 132
NATE 194
National Curriculum
  guidelines 69
  implementation 97
  planning 128
  policy documents 112
  requirements 1, 163
  resources 189
  writing 166
National Literacy Framework *see*
  Literacy Framework
A Necklace of Raindrops 32–5
negative time 143–4
new staff 109
New Zealand 16
newcomers 8
newsletters 55
non-fiction 14, 117, 192
non-mother tongue speakers
  101–2, 119, 154, 173
non-scheme books 20, 76
norm referenced tests 161
notebooks 120–1, 165, 170
notice boards 19, 48–50, 62, 80,
  82
nurseries 126, 137, 154
nursery rhymes 30–2, 89

objectives of policy documents
  112
observation 161, 165, 174, 178
OFSTED 109
onset 84
opportunities for assessment
  144–5
oral skills 6, 144
orientational perception 120
Oscar Got the Blame 24–30

other coordinators 9, 11, 16, 50,
  125
other subjects 97–100
overhead projectors (OHPs) 59,
  60–1
ownership 64, 69, 110, 116,
  168

paper 20, 169–70, 189
parents 6, 10, 20
  assessment 141, 150
  bedtime stories 73
  bookmarks 86
  consistency 114–15
  favourite books 81
  folders 170–1
  foundations 72
  home links 120–1
  information 71
  interviews 142
  planning 50
  policy documents 109, 112
  promotional projects 15
  reading 160, 164
  reports 180–3
  sharing information 55
  special needs 104
  target setting 158–9
  writing 168
partnerships 181
pencils 20, 189
pens 20, 189
performance indicators 153–4,
  162
Performance Indicators in
  Primary Schools (PIPS)
  150–2, 154
Peters, M. 90
philosophy 70, 111, 165
phonemic awareness 84–5,
  89–90, 103
phonics 129, 130
photographs 15
picnics 96
pilot projects 18

planning 126–37, 141
  budgets 55–6
  colleagues 12, 49
  Literacy Framework 95
  subject knowledge 70
  success 16–19
play 135–6, 173
playground duty 9
playscripts 146–7
poetry 14, 117
  assessment 148–9
  planning 129–30, 132
  resources 192
policy documents 109–25
portfolios 177–9, 182
positive approaches 9, 89, 115
positive time 143, 176
posters 19
pre-test stress 161
presentation
  of policy documents 122–3
  skills 50, 61–2
print
  awareness 15, 16
  environment 21, 120, 167, 180
  understanding 167
  walks 80, 116
programmes of study 1
progress 6, 164, 165
promotional projects 15
PTA 193
publication dates 188
punctuation 94, 122, 128–30, 166
punishment 175
pupil involvement *see* explicit learning

questionnaires 16
questions 19–20, 24, 61
  assessment 144–6
  curriculum sessions 181

Rat-a-Tat-Tat 89
Read, C. 88

reading
  achievement 160, 175
  ages 160
  computers 191
  consistency 114
  development 2
  evenings 55
  hour 55
  learning experiences 83–93
  other subjects 97
  parents' 180
  performance levels 153, 154
  planning 135, 137
  portfolios 178
  recommendations 122
  resources 192
  schemes 56, 142, 187, 189
  shared 144
  spaces 20
  target setting 156
  tests 161–2
Real Book debate 190
reciprocity 9
recommended reading 122
record-keeping 121, 141, 143, 178
recycling 187–8
reinforcement of practice 94–6
reports 142, 180–3
research 6, 71, 80
  assessment 142
  beliefs 83–4, 92
  policy documents 112
  resources 195
resources 121–2, 133
  achievement 169–70
  assessment 144
  management 187–95
responsibility 6
retelling 162
rhyme 164, 173, 192
rime 84
role of coordinators 5–7, 8–10, 56, 71
role models 119, 180
role play 17, 19, 135–7, 173

roots 8
Rosen, M. 93
Ross, T. 86
routines 131
running records 162

Sartre, J.-P. 74
SATs 155–9, 174, 176, 178
scaffolding 47, 166
School Development Plans 55, 125
science 125
scribing 21
seating 60
secondary schools 162
secretaries 9, 61
security 189–90
self-correction 167
self-image 169
Sendak, M. 86, 95
senior management 8, 114
sentence level 85, 145
settings for assessment 165
shared reading 145
shared writing 146
sharing information 50–6
short-term planning 131–4
siblings 74
signs 80, 96
Six Dinner Sid 96
skills 125
social interaction 78, 116
socialising 9
society 6
speaking 72, 134–5, 137
  see also talking
special needs 103–4, 119–20
speech marks 85
spelling 17, 84, 87–9
  achievement 166, 169
  classroom organisation 118
  computers 191
  confidence 124
  consistency 115
  folders 170

Have a Go books 170, 172, 178
  parents 181
  planning 129, 130
  portfolios 177
  target setting 157
  teachers 104
  visual 90
spontaneity 126
Spot books 80
staff development 50, 57–65, 71, 124–5
staff meetings 8, 58, 92, 111, 124–5
staffrooms 48–50, 59, 62, 93
standards 6, 24, 126
  assessment 174
  attainment 176
  target setting 159
  tests 161–3
starting out 10–14
stationery 121
statistical analysis 152
storage 56, 122, 170
  data 179
  equipment 189
  portfolios 178–9
story books 14
storytelling 85, 102, 180
storytime 50, 163–4
stress 175, 183
subject knowledge 70, 71
subject leaders 6, 7
subscriptions 92, 192
success 16–19, 115–16, 183
supermarkets 180
supply teachers 109
support 64–5, 72, 79, 176
syntax 85

Taiwan 176
taking stock 10
talking 77, 79, 97, 113
  achievement 172–4
  see also speaking
talking books 191

target setting 155–9
Teacher Training Agency (TTA)
    6, 7
teachers
    assessment 143–4
    child-centred learning 92–3
    confidence 124
    decision-making 142
    English as an additional
      language 101–2, 119
    environmental print 82–3
    foundations 75–7, 79
    Literacy Framework 104
    portfolios 179
    reading 114
    resources 193
    stress 175
    writing 115
Teddy Bears' Picnic 22–3
tests 144, 160–3, 165
text selection 85–6, 92–3
    achievement 163–4
    policy documents 117, 122
    resources 190–1, 192–3
thinking aloud 21
thinking skills 172–3
tick sheets 142–3
tidiness 81–2, 116
time 2, 49–50
    allocation 118–19
    evaluation 174
    management 121, 142, 143
timetables 19
Torrington 11
toy detectives 97–100
trials 179
Turbill 142
typewriters 20

UKRA 194
understanding print 167
United States of America (USA)
    76

verbal agreements 109
videos 193
visual perception 120
vocabulary 6, 21, 115, 118
    assessment 144, 146
    planning 129, 130, 135
Vygotsky, L. 77–8

Watanabe, S. 80
Waterland, L. 85
We're Going on a Bear Hunt 93
Where the Wild Things Are
    95–6
whole class assessment 145–9
Whole Language movement 76
Williams, S. 91, 92, 93
Wilson, D. 11
windows 59
Woodward, H. 143
word attack skills 84
worksheets 189
writing
    achievement 166–72, 175–6
    children 9
    classroom organisation 118
    computers 191
    consistency 115
    experiences 20
    folders 170–2
    learning experiences 83–93
    modelling 21–3
    other subjects 97
    parents 181
    planning 135, 137
    portfolios 177–8
    scaffolding 47
    shared 146
    skills 6
    spaces 20
    support 87
    target setting 156

Year 2 assessment 154–5